Yada, Yada,
Yada.com.org.edu.gov.email

Yada, Yada, Yada.com.org.edu.gov.email

What I learned on the WWW/Internet—Total Nonsense

Joan E. Miller

Writers Club Press
New York Lincoln Shanghai

Yada, Yada, Yada.com.org.edu.gov.email
What I learned on the WWW/Internet—Total Nonsense

Writers Club Press
an imprint of iUniverse, Inc.

For information address:
iUniverse, Inc.
2021 Pine Lake Road, Suite 100
Lincoln, NE 68512
www.iuniverse.com

The information contained herein is provided as a public service with the
understanding that the author makes no warranties, either expressed or
implied, concerning the accuracy, completeness, reliability, or suitability of the
information. Nor does the author warrant that the use of this information is
free of any claims of copyright infringement.

The author does not endorse any commercial providers or their products.

The opinions and information expressed throughout these pages are purely
those of the authors and intended for entertainment purposes only

ISBN: 0-595-10061-9

Printed in the United States of America

Dedicated to all the novice computer users & to my parents who have never even sat down at one.

CONTENTS

ACKNOWLEDGEMENTS

Thank you emailers and computer manufacturers for this informational and fun media.

LIST OF ABBREVIATIONS

.com	commercial
.org	organization
.gov	government
e	electronic (e-mail), (e-commerce), (e.trade)

LIST OF CONTRIBUTORS

Contributors include all the members of email anonymous

INTRODUCTION

Every time I open my emailbox there is another round of nonsense.

Did You Know.com

In English pubs, ale is ordered by pints and quarts. So in old England, when customers got unruly, the bartender would yell at them to mind their own pints and quarts and settle down. It's where we get the phrase "mind your P's and Q's."

Many years ago in England, pub frequenters had a whistle baked into the rim or handle of their ceramic cups. When they needed a refill, they used the whistle to get some service. "Wet your whistle," is the phrase inspired by this practice.

In Shakespeare's time, mattresses were secured on bed frames by ropes—when you pulled on the ropes the mattress tightened, making the bed firmer to sleep on. That's where the phrase, "good night, sleep tight" came from.

The sentence "The quick brown fox jumps over the lazy dog." uses every letter in the alphabet. (developed by Western Union to test telex/twx communications)

The only 15 letter word that can be spelled without repeating a letter is uncopyrightable.

When opossums are playing 'possum, they are not "playing" they actually pass out from sheer terror.

The Main Library at Indiana University sinks over an inch every year because when it was built the builder failed to take into consideration the weight of all the books that would occupy the building.

The term "the whole 9 yards" came from W.W.II fighter pilots in the Pacific. When arming their airplanes on the ground, the .50 caliber machine gun ammo belts measured exactly 27 feet, before being loaded into the fuselage. If the pilots fired all their ammo at a target, it got "the whole 9 yards".

The phrase "rule of thumb" is derived from an old English law which stated that you couldn't beat your wife with anything wider than your thumb.

An ostrich's eye is bigger than its brain.

The name Jeep came from the abbreviation used in the army for the "General Purpose" vehicle, G.P.

The cruise liner, Queen Elizabeth II, moves only six inches for each gallon of diesel that it burns.

Nutmeg is extremely poisonous if injected intravenously.

No NFL team which plays its home games in a domed stadium has ever won a Super Bowl.

The first toilet ever seen on television was on "Leave It To Beaver".

Only one person in two billion will live to be 116 or older.

In Cleveland, Ohio, it's illegal to catch mice without a hunting license.

It takes 3,000 cows to supply the NFL with enough leather for a year' supply of footballs.

Thirty-five percent of the people who use personal ads for dating are already married.

There are an average of 178 sesame seeds on a McDonald's Big Mac bun.

The world's termites outweigh the world's humans 10 to 1.

The 3 most valuable brand names on earth: Marlboro, Coca-Cola, and Budweiser, in that order.

When Heinz ketchup leaves the bottle, it travels at a rate of 25 miles per year.

Ten percent of the Russian government's income comes from the sale of vodka.

On average, 100 people choke to death on ball-point pens every year.

In 10 minutes, a hurricane releases more energy than all the world's nuclear weapons combined.

If you yelled for 8 years, 7 months and 6 days, you would have produced enough sound energy to heat one cup of coffee.

If you fart consistently for 6 years and 9 months, enough gas is produced to create the energy of an atomic bomb.

The human heart creates enough pressure when it pumps blood out to the body to squirt blood 30 feet.

Banging your head against a wall uses 150 calories an hour.

Humans and dolphins are the only species that have sex for pleasure.

On average people fear spiders more than they do death.

The strongest muscle in the body is the TONGUE.

It's impossible to sneeze with your eyes open.

You can't kill yourself by holding your breath.

Americans on the average eat 18 acres of pizza every day.

Every time you lick a stamp, you're consuming 1/10 of a calorie.

Did you know that you are more likely to be killed by a champagne cork than by a poisonous spider?

Right-handed people live, on average, nine years longer than left-handed people do.

In ancient Egypt, Priests plucked EVERY hair from their bodies, including their eyebrows and eyelashes.

A pig's orgasm lasts for 30 minutes.

A crocodile cannot stick its tongue out.

The ant can lift 50 times its own weight, can pull 30 times its own weight and always falls over on its right side when intoxicated.

Polar bears are left handed.

The catfish has over 27,000 taste buds, that makes the catfish rank #1 for animal having the most taste buds.

The flea can jump 350 times its body length, that is like a human jumping the length of a football field.

A cockroach will live nine days without its head before it starves to death.

The male praying mantis cannot copulate while its head is attached to its body. The female initiates sex by ripping the males head off.

Some lions mate over 50 times a day.

Butterflies taste with their feet.

Elephants are the only animals that can't jump.
A cat's urine glows under a blacklight.
An ostrich's eye is bigger than it's brain.
Starfishes haven't got brains.
After reading all these, all I can say is...DAMN PIGS

RANDOM FUNNY FACTS.COM

* Gilligan of Gilligan's Island had a first name that was only used once, on the never-aired pilot show. His first name was Willy.

* Dr. Seuss and Kurt Vonnegut went to college together. They were even in the same fraternity, where Seuss decorated the fraternity house walls with drawings of his strange characters.

* The Lees Nessman character on the TV series WKRP in Cincinnati wore a Band-Aid in every episode. Either on himself, his glasses, or his clothing.

* John Larroquette of "Night Court" and "The John Larroquette Show" was the narrator of "The Texas Chainsaw Massacre."

* Beelzebub, another name for the devil, is Hebrew for "Lord of the Flies", and this is where the book's title comes from.

* The term "devil's advocate" comes from the Roman Catholic Church. When deciding if someone should be sainted, a devil's advocate is always appointed to give an alternative view.

* Before Prohibition, Schlitz Brewery owned more property in Chicago than anyone else, except The Catholic Church.

* It is believed that Shakespeare was 46 around the time that the King James Version of the Bible was written. In Psalms 46, the 46th word from the first word is 'shake' and the 46th word from the last word is 'spear'.

* In 1986 Danny Heep became the first player in a World Series to be a designated hitter (DH) with the initials "D.H.".

* In the four major US professional sports, (Baseball, Basketball, Football, and Hockey), there are only seven teams whose nicknames do not end with an "S:" Basketball: The Miami Heat, The Utah Jazz, The Orlando Magic. Baseball: The Boston Red Sox, The Chicago White Sox. Hockey: The Colorado Avalanche, The Tampa Bay Lightning. Football: None.

* In 1963, baseball pitcher Gaylord Perry remarked, "They'll put a man on the moon before I hit a home run." On July 20, 1969, a few hours after Neil Armstrong set foot on the moon, Gaylord Perry hit his first, and only, home run.

* Kermit the Frog is left-handed.

* The lifespan of a taste bud is ten days.

* Non-dairy creamer is flammable.

* The dial tone of a normal telephone is in the key of "F".

* If you put a raisin in a glass of champagne, it will keep floating to the top and sinking to the bottom.

Rubber bands last longer when refrigerated.

Peanuts are one of the ingredients of dynamite.

The national anthem of Greece has 158 verses.

No one in Greece has memorized all 158 verses.

There are 293 ways to make change for a dollar.

The average person's left hand does 56% of the typing.

The shark is the only fish that can blink with both eyes.

There are more chickens than people in the world.

Two-thirds of the world's eggplant is grown in New Jersey.

The longest one-syllable word in the English language is "screeched."

On a Canadian two dollar bill, the flag flying over the Parliament Building is an American flag.

All of the clocks in the movie "Pulp Fiction" are stuck on 4:20.

No word in the English language rhymes with month, orange, silver or purple.

"Dreamt" is the only English word that ends in the letters "mt."

All 50 states are listed across the top of the Lincoln Memorial on the back of the $5 bill.

Almonds are a member of the peach family.

Winston Churchill was born in a ladies' room during a dance.

Maine is the only state whose name is just one syllable.

There are only four words in the English language which end in "dous": tremendous, horrendous, stupendous, and hazardous.

Los Angeles's full name is "El Pueblo de Nuestra Senora la Reina de los Angeles de Porciuncula"-and can be abbreviated to 3.63% of its size: "L.A."

A cat has 32 muscles in each ear.

Tigers have striped skin, not just striped fur.

In most advertisements, including newspapers, the time displayed on a watch is 10:10.

Al Capone's business card said he was a used furniture dealer.

The only real person to be a Pez head was Betsy Ross.

When the University of Nebraska Cornhuskers play football at home, the stadium becomes the state's third largest city.

The characters Bert and Ernie on Sesame Street were named after Bert the cop and Ernie the taxi driver in Frank Capra's "Its A Wonderful Life."

A dragonfly has a lifespan of 24 hours.

A goldfish has a memory span of three seconds.

A dime has 118 ridges around the edge.

On an American one-dollar bill, there is an owl in the upper left-hand corner of the "1" encased in the "shield" and a spider hidden in the front upper right-hand corner.

The giant squid has the largest eyes in the world.

In England, the Speaker of the House is not allowed to speak.

The name for Oz in the "Wizard of Oz" was thought up when the creator, Frank Baum, looked at his filing cabinet and saw A-N, and O-Z, hence "Oz."

The microwave was invented after a researcher walked by a radar tube and a chocolate bar melted in his pocket.

Mr. Rogers is an ordained minister.

John Lennon's first girlfriend was named Thelma Pickles.

The average person falls asleep in seven minutes.

There are 336 dimples on a regulation golf ball.

"Stewardesses" is the longest word that is typed with only the left hand.

Amazingly, 11/19/1999, was the last day of your life that all the digits of the date were completely odd.

Of course, with modern science you might be able to make it to the next odd date, which will be on 1/1/3111, but don't count on it. A more attainable goal might be to live for the next all even digit day. This February we'll have the first day after over a millennium where all the digits are even, 2/2/2000. The last time this occurred was in 8/8/888. You will probably have a lot of even days, but this day was your last odd day.

ACTUAL ANSWERING MACHINE MESSAGE.COM

* My wife and I can't come to the phone right now, but if you'll leave your name and number, we'll get back to you as soon as we're finished.

* A is for academics, B is for beer. One of those reasons is why we're not here. So leave a message.

* Hi. This is John: If you are the phone company, I already sent the money. If you are my parents, please send money. If you are my financial aid institution, you didn't lend me enough money. If you are my friends, you owe me money. If you are a female, don't worry, I have plenty of money.

* Hi. Now you say something.

* Hi, I'm not home right now but my answering machine is, so you can talk to it instead. Wait for the beep.

* Hello. I am David's answering machine. What are you?

* (From Japanese friend) He-lo! This is Sa-to, If you leave message, I call you soon. If you leave "sexy" message, I call sooner!

* Hi. John's answering machine is broken. This is his refrigerator. Please speak very slowly, and I'll stick your message to myself with one of these magnets.

* Hello, you are talking to a machine. I am capable of receiving messages.

* My owners do not need siding, windows, or a hot tub, and their carpets are clean. They give to charity through their office and do not need their picture taken. If you're still with me, leave your name and number and they will get back to you.

* This is not an answering machine, this is a telepathic thought recording device. After the tone, think about your name, your reason for calling and a number where I can reach you, and I'll think about returning your call.

* Hi. I am probably home, I'm just avoiding someone I don't like. Leave me a message, and if I don't call back, it's you.

* Hi, this is George. I'm sorry I can't answer the phone right now. Leave a message, and then wait by your phone until I call you back.

* If you are a burglar, then we're probably home cleaning our weapons right now and can't come to the phone. Otherwise, we probably aren't home and it's safe to leave us a message.

* Please leave a message. However, you have the right to remain silent. Everything you say will be recorded and will be used by us.

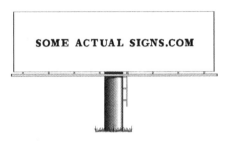

SOME ACTUAL SIGNS.COM

In the front yard of a funeral home, "Drive carefully, we'll wait."

On an electrician's truck, "Let us remove your shorts."

Outside a radiator repair shop, "Best place in town to take a leak."

In a nonsmoking area, "If we see you smoking, we will assume you are on fire and take appropriate action."

On a maternity room door, "Push, Push, Push."

On a front door, "Everyone on the premises is a vegetarian except the dog."

At an optometrist's office, "If you don't see what you're looking for, you've come to the right place."

On a taxidermist's window, "We really know our stuff."

On a butcher's window, "Let me meat your needs."

On a fence, "Salesmen welcome. Dog food is expensive."

At a car dealership, "The best way to get back on your feet—miss a car payment."

Outside a muffler shop, "No appointment necessary. We'll hear you coming."

In a dry cleaner's emporium, "Drop your pants here."

On a desk in a reception room, "We shoot every 3rd salesman, and the 2nd one just left."

In a veterinarian's waiting room, "Be back in 5 minutes. Sit! Stay!"

At the electric company, "We would be delighted if you send in your bill. However, if you don't, you will be."

In a Beauty Shop, "Dye now!"

On the side of a garbage truck, "We've got what it takes to take what you've got."(Burglars please copy.)

In a restaurant window, "Don't stand there and be hungry, come in and get fed up."

Inside a bowling alley, "Please be quiet. We need to hear a pin drop."

In a cafeteria, "Shoes are required to eat in the cafeteria. Socks can eat any place they want."

OFFICE INSPIRATIONAL POSTERS.COM

Rome did not create a great empire by having meetings, they did it by killing all those who opposed them.

If you can stay calm, while all around you is chaos…then you probably haven't completely understood the seriousness of the situation.

"WORK" is a four-letter word.

Doing a job RIGHT the first time gets the job done.

Doing the job WRONG fourteen times gives you job security.

We will do no work before its nine.

Eagles may soar, but weasels don't get sucked into jet engines.

We put the "k" in "kwality."

Artificial Intelligence is no match for Natural Stupidity

A person who smiles in the face of adversity…probably has a scapegoat.

Plagiarism saves time.

If at first you don't succeed, try management.

Never put off until tomorrow what you can avoid altogether.

TEAMWORK means never having to take all the blame yourself.

The beatings will continue until morale improves.

IPTs: Never underestimate the power of very stupid people in large groups.

We waste time, so you don't have to.

Hang in there, retirement is only thirty years away!

Go the extra mile.

It makes your boss look like an incompetent slacker.

A snooze button is a poor substitute for no alarm clock at all.

When the going gets tough, the tough take a coffee break.

INDECISION is the key to FLEXIBILITY.

Succeed in spite of management.

Aim Low, Reach Your Goals, Avoid Disappointment.

We waste more time by 8:00 in the morning than other companies do all day.

You pretend to work, and we'll pretend to pay you.

Work: It isn't just for sleeping anymore.

Bumper Stickers.com

It doesn't matter if you pick your nose...Its where you put the boogers that counts!

People are more violently opposed to fur than leather because it is easier to harass rich women than motorcycle gangs.

Remember when sex was safe and motorcycles were dangerous.

Forget about world peace, visualize using your turn signal.

It's time to change the air in your head.

EARTH FIRST! We'll strip-mine the other planets later.

Jesus is coming, everyone look busy.

A bartender is just a pharmacist with a limited inventory.

Horn broken, watch for finger.

My kid had sex with your honor student.

If at first you do succeed, try not to look astonished.

Help wanted telepath: you know where to apply

I.R.S.: We've got what it takes to take what you've got.

Jesus loves you...everyone else thinks you're an asshole.

I'm just driving this way to piss you off.

Reality is a crutch for people who can't handle drugs.

Keep honking, I'm reloading.

Hang up and drive.

Lord save me from your followers.

Ask me about microwaving cats for fun and profit

I said "no" to drugs, but they just wouldn't listen.

Friends don't let Friends drive Naked

If we aren't supposed to eat animals, why are they made of meat?

Lottery: A tax on people who are bad at math.

Friends help you move. Real friends help you move bodies.

Diplomacy is the art of saying 'Nice doggie!'…till you can find a rock.

Sex on television can't hurt you unless you fall off.

Your kid may be an honors student, but you're still an idiot.

Learn from your parents' mistakes—use birth control.

We have enough youth, how about a fountain of Smart?

He who laughs last thinks slowest.

It IS as bad as you think, and they ARE out to get you.

Auntie Em, Hate you, hate Kansas, taking the dog. Dorothy.

Time is what keeps everything from happening at once.

I get enough exercise just pushing my luck.

All men are idiots, and I married their King.

Jack Kevorkian for White House Physician.

Montana—At least our cows are sane!

Women who seek to be equal to men lack ambition.

Where there's a will, I want to be in it.

OK, who stopped payment on my reality check?

Few women admit their age; Fewer men act it.

I don't suffer from insanity, I enjoy every minute of it.

Hard work has a future payoff. Laziness pays off NOW.

Time is the best teacher, unfortunately it kills all of its students.

Some people are only alive because it is illegal to kill.

Warning: Dates in Calendar are closer than they appear.

Always remember you're unique, just like everyone else.

Very funny Scotty, now beam down my clothes.

Be nice to your kids. They'll choose your nursing home.

There are 3 kinds of people: those who can count & those who can't.

Why is 'abbreviation' such a long word?

GRAFFITI.COM

Friends don't let friends take home ugly men
~~~Women's restroom, Starboard, Dewey Beach, DE
Remember, it's not, "How high are you?" it's "Hi, how are you?"
~~~ Rest stop off Route 81, West Virginia.
No matter how good she looks, some other guy is sick and tired of putting up with her shit.
~~~Men's Room, Linda's Bar and Grill, Chapel Hill, North Carolina.
To do is to be—Descartes; To be is to do—Voltaire; Do be do be do—Frank Sinatra.
~~~Men's restroom, Greasewood Flats, Scottsdale, Arizona.
Make love, not war.-Hell, do both, get married!
~~~Women's restroom, The Filling Station, Bozeman, Montana.
A Woman's Rule of Thumb: If it has tires or testicles, you're going to have trouble with it.
~~~Women's restroom, Dick's Last Resort, Dallas, Texas
Express Lane: Five beers or less
~~~Sign over one of the urinals, Ed Debevic's, Beverly Hills, Ca.
You're too good for him.
~~~Sign over mirror in Women's restroom, Ed Debevics, Beverly Hill, Ca.
No wonder you always go home alone.
~~~Sign over mirror in Men's restroom, Ed Debevic's, Beverly Hills, Ca.
The best way to a man's heart is to saw his breast plate open.
~~~Women's restroom, Murphy's, Champaign, IL
If you voted for Clinton in the last election, you can't take a dump here. Your asshole is in Washington.
~~~Men's room Outback Steakhouse, Tacoma, Washington
Beauty is only a light switch away.

~~~Perkins Library, Duke University, Durham, North Carolina.

I've decided that to raise my grades I must lower my standards.

~~~Houghton Library, Harvard University, Cambridge, Massachusetts.

If life is a waste of time, and time is a waste of life, then let's all get wasted together and have the time of our lives.

~~~Armand's Pizza, Washington, DC

God made pot. Man made beer. Who do you trust?

~~~The Irish Times, Washington, DC

It's hard to make a comeback when you haven't been anywhere.

~~~Written in the dust on the back of a bus, Wickenburg, Arizona.

If voting could really change things, it would be illegal.

~~~Revolution Books, New York, New York

Don't trust anything that bleeds for 5 days and doesn't die.

~~~Men's restroom, Murphy's, Champaign, IL

What are you looking up on the wall for? The joke is in your hands.

~~~Men's restroom, Lynagh's, Lexington, KY

Sign? Bumper Stickers? Poster?Grafitti? You Decide.com

Save the trees Wipe your butt with an owl.

Honk if you've never seen an Uzi fired from a car window.

Seen on the back of a biker's vest: If you can read this, my wife fell off.

If you can read this, please flip me back.

Remember folks: Stop lights timed for 35 mph are also timed for 70 mph.

Impotence: Nature's way of saying "No hard feelings"

Don't be sexist—broads hate that!

Who lit the fuse on your tampon?

Fight Crime: Shoot Back!

Please tell your pants it's not polite to point.

A pat on the back is only a few centimeters from a kick in the ass.

Never raise your hands to your kids; it leaves your groin unprotected.

Feel safe tonight Sleep with a cop.

GUYS: No shirt, no service. GALS: No shirt, no charge.

Heart Attacks God's Revenge For Eating His Animal Friends

We have enough youth, how about a fountain of smart?

Boldly going nowhere.

Cat: The other white meat.

CAUTION—Driver legally blonde.

Eat Well, Stay Fit, Die Anyway.

He's not dead, He's electroencephalographically challenged.

If at first you don't succeed, skydiving is not for you.

If you can't dazzle them with brilliance, riddle them with bullets.

If you lived in your car, you'd be home by now.

WARNING! Driver only carries $20.00 in ammunition.

Your ridiculous little opinion has been noted.

I don't suffer from insanity, I enjoy every minute of it.

I Work Hard Because Millions On Welfare Depend on Me!

Some people are alive only because it's illegal to kill them.

I used to have a handle on life, but it broke.

Don't take life too seriously, you won't get out alive.

You're just jealous because the voices only talk to me.

I got a gun for my wife, best trade I ever made.

So you're a feminist…Isn't that cute!

Earth is the insane asylum for the universe.

I'm not a complete idiot, some parts are missing.

Earth first…we'll mine the other planets later.

I want to die in my sleep like my grandfather…Not screaming and yelling like the passengers in his car.

God must love stupid people, he made so many.

The gene pool could use a little chlorine.

Who pissed in your gene pool?

It IS as BAD as you think, and they ARE out to get you.

I took an IQ test and the results were negative.

It's lonely at the top, but you eat better.

Give me ambiguity or give me something else.

I know what you're thinking, and you should be ashamed of yourself.

We are born naked, wet and hungry. Then things get worse.

Lottery: A tax on people who are bad at math.

Very funny, Scotty. Now beam down my clothes.

Consciousness: that annoying time between naps.

Ever stop to think, and forget to start again?

I'm Out Of Bed And Dressed; What More Do You Want?

(Around a picture of dandelions): I Fought the Lawn and the Lawn Won.

So Many Men, So Few Who Can Afford Me

God Made Us Sisters; Prozac Made Us Friends

If They Don't Have Chocolate in Heaven, I Ain't Going.

At My Age, I've Seen It All, Done It All, Heard It All . I Just Can't
Remember It All.

My Mother Is a Travel Agent for Guilt Trips

(Spotted at a gay pride parade): My Son Just Came Out of the Closet and
All I Got Was This Lousy T-shirt.

Senior Citizen: Give Me My Damn Discount

Princess, Having Had Sufficient Experience With Princes, Seeks Frog

What If the Hokey Pokey Really IS What It's All About?

Coffee, Chocolate, Men…Some Things Are Just Better Rich

Don't Treat Me Any Differently Than You Would the Queen

If You Want Breakfast in Bed, Sleep in the Kitchen

Get a New Car for Your Spouse. It'll Be a Great Trade.

It's Hard to Be Nostalgic When You Can't Remember Anything.

Dinner Is Ready When the Smoke Alarm Goes Off.

A City Is a Large Community Where People Are Lonesome Together.

In America, Anyone Can Be President. That's One of the Risks You Take.

Sarcasmisms. com

1. And your crybaby whiny-assed opinion would be.?
   2. Do I look like a people person?
   3. This isn't an office. It's Hell with fluorescent lighting.
   4. I started out with nothing & still have most of it left.
   5. Sarcasm is just one more service we offer.
   6. If I throw a stick, will you leave?
   7. You!…Off my planet!
   8. Does your train of thought have a caboose?
   9. Did the aliens forget to remove your anal probe?
   10. Errors have been made. Others will be blamed.
   11. A PBS mind in an MTV world.
   12. Allow me to introduce my selves.
   13. Whatever kind of look you were going for, you missed.
   14. Well, this day was a total waste of makeup.
   15. See no evil, hear no evil, date no evil.
   16. Are those your eyeballs? I found them in my cleavage.
   17. Not all men are annoying. Some are dead.
   18. I'm trying to imagine you with a personality.
   19. A cubicle is just a padded cell without a door.
   20. Stress is when you wake up screaming & you realize you haven't fallen asleep yet.
   21. Can I trade this job for what's behind door 1?
   22. Too many freaks, not enough circuses.
   23. Nice perfume. Must you marinate in it?
   24. Chaos, panic, & disorder—my work here is done.
   25. How do I set a laser printer to stun?
   26. I thought I wanted a career, turns out I just wanted paychecks.

27. Here I am! Now what are your other two wishes?
28. I just want revenge. Is that so wrong?
29. Ambivalent? Well, yes and no.
30. Earth is full. Go home.
31. I thought I wanted a career, turns out I just wanted paychecks.
32. Meandering to a different drummer.
33. I majored in liberal arts. Will that be for here or to go?

EXCUSES.COM

These are actual excuse notes from parents (including spelling)

My son is under a doctor's care and should not take P.E. today. Please execute him.

Please excuse Lisa for being absent. She was sick and I had her shot.

Dear School: Please excuse John being absent on Jan. 28, 29, 30, 31, 32 and 33.

Please excuse Gloria from Jim Today. She is administrating.

Please excuse Roland from Pl E. for a few days. yesterday he fell out of a tree and misplaced his hip.

John has been absent because he had two teeth taken out of his face.

Carlos was absent yesterday because he was playing football. He was hurt in the growing parts.

Megan could not come t school toad because she has been bothered by very close veins.

Chris will not be in school cu he has an acre in his side.

Please excuse Ray Friday from school. He has very loose vowels.

Please excuse Tommy for being absent yesterday. He had diarrhea and his boots leak.

Irving was absent yesterday because he missed his bust.

Please excuse Jimmy for being. It was his father's fault.

Please excuse Jennifer for missing school yesterday. We forgot to get the Sunday paper off the porch, and when we found it Monday, we thought it was Sunday.

Sally won't be in school a week from Friday. We have to attend her funeral.

My daughter was absent yesterday because she was tired. She spent a weekend with the Marines.

Please excuse Jason for being absent yesterday. He had a cold and could not breed well.

Please excuse Mary or being absent yesterday. She was in bed with gramps.

Please excuse Burma, she has been sick and under the doctor.

Maryann was absent December 11-16, because she had a fever, sore throat, headache and upset stomach. Her sister way also sick, fever and sore throat, her brother had a low grade fever and ached all over. I wasn't the best either. sore throat and fever. There must be something going around her father, even got hot last night.

The Facts of Life.com

1. The two most common elements in the universe are hydrogen and stupidity.
2. If at first you don't succeed, skydiving is not for you.
3. Money can't buy happiness, but it sure makes misery easier to live with.
4. Deja Moo: The feeling that you've heard this bull before.
5. Psychiatrists say that 1 of 4 people are mentally ill. Check 3 friends. If they're OK, you're it.
6. Nothing in the known universe travels faster than a bad check.
7. A truly wise man never plays leap-frog with a unicorn.
8. It has recently been discovered that research causes cancer in rats.
9. Always remember to pillage BEFORE you burn.
10. If you are given an open-book exam, you will forget your book.
11. COROLLARY: If you are given a take-home test, you will forget where you live.
12. The trouble with doing something right the first time is that nobody appreciates how difficult it was.
13. It may be that your sole purpose in life is simply to serve as a warning to others.
14. Paul's Law: You can't fall off the floor.
15. The average woman would rather have beauty than brains, because the average man can see better than he can think.
16. Clothes make the man. Naked people have little or no influence on society.
17. Vital papers will demonstrate their vitality by moving from where you left them to where you can't find them.
18. Law of Probability Dispersal: Whatever it is that hits the fan will not be evenly distributed.

WORDS.COM

INTERESTING IF YOU EVER WONDERED WHERE CERTAIN EXPRESSIONS CAME FROM.

Life in the 1500's:

Most people got married in June because they took their yearly bath in May and were still smelling pretty good by June. However, they were starting to smell, so brides carried a bouquet of flowers to hide the b.o.

Baths equaled a big tub filled with hot water. The man of the house had the privilege of the nice clean water, then all the other sons and men, then the women and finally the children. Last of all the babies. By then the water was so dirty you could actually loose someone in it. Hence the saying, "Don't throw the baby out with the bath water."

Houses had thatched roofs. Thick straw, piled high, with no wood underneath. It was the only place for animals to get warm, so all the pets...dogs, cats and other small animals, mice, rats, bugs lived in the roof. When it rained it became slippery and sometimes the animals would slip and fall off the roof. Hence the saying, "It's raining cats and dogs."

There was nothing to stop things from falling into the house. This posed a real problem in the bedroom where bugs and other droppings could really mess up your nice clean bed. So, they found if they made beds with big posts and hung a sheet over the top, it addressed that problem. Hence those beautiful big 4 poster beds with canopies.

The floor was dirt. Only the wealthy had something other than dirt, hence the saying "dirt poor." The wealthy had slate floors which would get slippery in the winter when wet. So they spread thresh on the floor to help keep their footing. As the winter wore on they kept adding more thresh until when you opened the door it would all start slipping outside. A piece of wood was placed at the entry way. Hence a "thresh hold."

They cooked in the kitchen in a big kettle that always hung over the fire. Every day they lit the fire and added things to the pot. They mostly ate vegetables and didn't get much meat. They would eat the stew for dinner leaving leftovers in the pot to get cold overnight and then start over the next day. Sometimes the stew had food in it that had been in there for a month. Hence the rhyme: peas porridge hot, peas porridge cold, peas porridge in he pot nine days old."

Sometimes they could obtain pork and would feel really special when that happened. When company came over, they would bring out some bacon and hang it to show it off. It was a sign of wealth and that a man "could really bring home the bacon." They would cut off a little to share with guests and would all sit around and "chew the fat."

Those with money had plates made of pewter. Food with a high acid content caused some of the lead to leach onto the food. This happened most often with tomatoes, so they stopped eating tomatoes for 400 years.

Most people didn't have pewter plates, but had trenchers—a piece of wood with the middle scooped out like a bowl. Trenchers were never washed and a lot of times worms got into the wood. After eating off wormy trenchers, they would get "trench mouth."

Bread was divided according to status. Workers got the burnt bottom of the loaf, the family got the middle, and guests got the top, or the "upper crust."

Lead cups were used to drink ale or whiskey. The combination would sometimes knock them out for a couple of days. Someone walking along the road would take them for dead and prepare them for burial. They were laid out on the kitchen table for a couple of days and the family would gather around and eat and drink and wait and see if they would wake up. Hence the custom of holding a "wake."

England is old and small and they started running out of places to bury people. So, they would dig up coffins and would take their bones to a house and reuse the grave. In reopening these coffins, one out of 25 coffins were found to have scratch marks on the inside and they realized they had been burying people alive. So they thought they would tie a string on their wrist and lead it through the coffin and up through the ground and tie it to a bell. Someone would have to sit out in the graveyard all night to listen for the bell. Hence on the "graveyard shift" they would know that someone was "saved by the bell" or he was a "dead ringer."

SCRABBLE.COM

The following are exceptionally clever. Someone out there either has way too much time to waste or is deadly at Scrabble.com

When you rearrange the letters:

Dormitory	Dirty Room
Evangelist	Evil's Agent
Desperation	A Rope Ends It
The Morse Code	Here Come Dots
Slot Machines	Cash Lost in 'em
Animosity	Is No Amity
Mother-in-law	Woman Hitler
Snooze Alarms	Alas! No More Z's
Alec Guinness	Genuine Class
Semolina	Is No Meal
The Public Art Galleries	Large Picture Halls, I Bet
A Decimal Point	I'm a Dot in Place
The Earthquakes	That Queer Shake
Eleven plus two	Twelve plus one
Contradiction	Accord not in it

WHY ENGLISH IS SO HARD TO LEARN.EDU

We must polish the Polish furniture.
   He could lead if he would get the lead out.
   The farm was used to produce produce.
   The dump was so full that it had to refuse more refuse.
   The soldier decided to desert in the desert.
   This was a good time to present the present.
   (And this last could mean "gift" or "era of time ")
   A bass was painted on the head of the bass drum.
   When shot at, the dove dove into the bushes.
   I did not object to the object.
   The insurance was invalid for the invalid.
   The bandage was wound around the wound.
   There was a row among the oarsmen about how to row.
   They were too close to the door to close it.
   The buck does funny things when the does are present.
   They sent a sewer down to stitch the tear in the sewer line.
   To help with planting, the farmer taught his sow to sow.
   The wind was too strong to wind the sail.
   After a number of injections my jaw got number.
   Upon seeing the tear in my clothes I shed a tear.
   I had to subject the subject to a series of tests.
   How can I intimate this to my most intimate friend?

MERGERS.COM

Are your investments in order? Below are some of the latest rumors from Wall Street. In the wake of the AOL/Time Warner deal, here are the latest mergers we can expect to see.com

Hale Business Systems, Mary Kay Cosmetics, Fuller Brush, and W.R. Grace Company merge to become Hale Mary Fuller Grace.

Polygram Records, Warner Brothers, and Keebler Crackers merge to become Polly-Warner-Cracker.

3M and Goodyear merge to become MMMGood.

John Deere and Abitibi-Price merge to become Deere Abi.

Zippo Manufacturing, Audi Motors, Dofasco, and Dakota Mining merge to become Zip Audi Do Da.

Honeywell, Imasco, and Home Oil merge to become Honey I'm Home.

Denison Mines, and Alliance and Metal Mining merge to become Mine All Mine.

Federal Express and UPS merge to become FED UP.

Xerox and Wurlitzer will merge and begin manufacturing reproductive organs.

Fairchild Electronics and Honeywell Computers will merge and become Fairwell Honeychild.

3M, J.C. Penney and the Canadian Opera Company will merge and become 3 Penney Opera.

Knott's Berry Farm & National Organization of Women will merge and become Knott NOW!

Word Whys?.edu

1. Is it good if a vacuum really sucks?
2. Why is the third hand on the watch called the second hand?
3. If a word is misspelled in the dictionary, how would we ever know?
4. If Webster wrote the first dictionary, where did he find the words?
5. Why does "slow down" and "slow up" mean the same thing?
6. Why does "fat chance" and "slim chance" mean the same thing?
7. Why do "tug" boats push their barges?
8. Why do we sing "Take me out to the ball game" when we are already there?
9. Why are they called "stands" when they are made for sitting?
10. Why is it called "after dark" when it really is "after light"?
11. Doesn't "expecting the unexpected" make the unexpected expected?
12. Why is "phonics" not spelled the way it sounds?
13. If work is so terrific, why do they have to pay you to do it?
14. If all the world is a stage, where is the audience sitting?
15. If love is blind, why is lingerie so popular?
16. If you are cross-eyed and have dyslexia, can you read all right?
17. Why is bra singular and panties plural?
18. Why do you press harder on the buttons of a remote control when you know the batteries are dead?
19. Why do we put suits in garment bags and garments in a suitcase?
20. How come abbreviated is such a long word?
21. Why do we wash bath towels? Aren't we clean when we use them?
22. Why doesn't glue stick to the inside of the bottle?
23. Why do they call it a TV set when you only have one?
24. If you mixed vodka with orange juice and milk of magnesia, would you get a Phillip's Screwdriver?

25. Why do we say something is out of whack? What is a whack?
26. When someone asks you, "A penny for your thoughts," and you put your two cents in, what happens to the other penny?
27. Why is the man who invests all your money called a broker?
28. Why do croutons come in airtight packages? It's just stale bread to begin with.
29. When cheese gets its picture taken, what does it say?
30. Why is a person who plays the piano called a pianist, but a person who drives a race car not called a racist?
31. Why are a wise man and a wise guy opposites?
32. Why do overlook and oversee mean opposite things?
33. If horrific means to make horrible, does terrific mean to make terrible?
34. Why isn't 11 pronounced onety one?
35. "I am " is reportedly the shortest sentence in the English language. Could it be that "I do" is the longest sentence?
36. If you take an Oriental person and spin him around several times, does he become disoriented?
37. If people from Poland are called "Poles," why aren't people from Holland called "Holes"?
38. Why do they call it Rush Hour when nothing moves?
39. Why is there an Interstate highway in Hawaii?

~   ~   ~   ~   ~

If lawyers are disbarred and clergymen defrocked, doesn't it follow that electricians can be delighted, musicians denoted, cowboys deranged, models deposed and dry cleaners depressed? Laundry workers could decrease, eventually becoming depressed and depleted!

Even more, bed makers will be debunked, baseball players will be debased, landscapers will be deflowered, bulldozer operators will be degraded, organ donors will be delivered, software engineers will be detested, the BVD company will be debriefed, and even musical composers will eventually decompose.

On a more positive note though, perhaps we can hope politicians will be devoted.gov.

WORDS TO THE WISE.EDU

This guy goes into a restaurant for a Christmas breakfast while in his home town for the holidays. After looking over the menu he says, "I'll just have the Eggs Benedict." His order comes a while later and it's served on a big, shiny hubcap. He asks the waiter, "What's with the hubcap?" The waiter sings, "There's no plate like chrome for the hollandaise!"

Did you hear about the Buddhist who refused his dentist's Novocain during root canal work? He wanted to transcend dental medication.

A group of chess enthusiasts checked into a hotel and were standing in the lobby discussing their recent tournament victories. After about an hour, the manager came out of the office and asked them to disperse. "But why?" they asked, as they moved off. "Because," he said, "I can't stand chess nuts boasting in an open foyer."

A doctor made it his regular habit to stop off at a bar for a hazelnut daiquiri on his way home. The bartender knew of his habit, and would always have the drink waiting at precisely 5:03 p.m. One afternoon, as the end of the work day approached, the bartender was dismayed to find that he was out of hazelnut extract. Thinking quickly, he threw together a daiquiri made with hickory nuts and set it on the bar. The doctor came in at his regular time, took one sip of the drink and exclaimed, "This isn't a hazelnut daiquiri!" "No, I'm sorry," replied the bartender, "it's a hickory daiquiri, doc."

The Boston Symphony was performing Beethoven's Ninth. In the piece, there's a long passage about 20 minutes during which the bass violinists have nothing to do.

Rather than sit around the whole time looking stupid, some bassists decided to sneak offstage and go to the tavern next door for a quick one. After slamming several beers in quick succession (as bass violinists are prone to do), one of them looked at his watch. "Hey! We need to get back!" "No need to panic," said a fellow bassist. "I thought we might need some extra time, so I tied the last few pages of the conductor's score together with string. It'll take him a few minutes to get it untangled." A few moments later they staggered back to the concert hall and took their places in the orchestra. About this time, a member of the audience noticed the conductor seemed a bit edgy and said as much to her companion. "Well, of course," said her companion. "Don't you see? It's the bottom of the Ninth, the score is tied, and the bassists are loaded."

and last but certainly not least.

Mahatma Ghandi walked barefoot everywhere, to the point that his feet became quite thick and hard. He also was quite a spiritual person. Even when he was not on a hunger strike, he did not eat much and became quite thin and frail. Furthermore, due to his diet, he wound up with very bad breath. Therefore, he came to be know as a...(get ready....)

"Super callused fragile mystic plagued with halitosis."

Hows, Whats and Whys.com

How do crazy people go through the forest? They take the psycho path.

How do you get holy water? Boil the hell out of it.

What did the fish say when it hit a concrete wall? "Dam!"

What do Eskimos get from sitting on the ice too long? Polaroids.

What do you call a boomerang that doesn't work? A stick.

What do you call cheese that isn't yours? Nacho Cheese.

What do you call Santa's helper? Subordinate Clauses.

What do you call four bullfighters in quicksand? Quatro sinko.

What do you get from a pampered cow? Spoiled milk.

What do you get when you cross a snowman with a vampire? Frostbite.

What lies at the bottom of the ocean and twitches? A nervous wreck.

What's the difference between roast beef and pea soup? Anyone can roast beef.

Why do gorillas have big nostrils? Because they have big fingers.

Why don't blind people like to sky dive? Because it scares the heck out of the dog.

What kind of coffee was served on the Titanic? Sanka.

What is the difference between a Harley and a Hoover? The location of the dirt bag.

Why do pilgrim's pants always fall down? Because they wear their belt buckle on their hat.

What's the difference between a bad golfer and a bad skydiver?

A bad golfer goes, WHACK! "Damn."

A bad skydiver goes, "Damn." WHACK!

What do you call a man with a car on his head? Jack

How do you catch a unique rabbit? Unique up on it!

How do you catch a tame rabbit? Tame way, unique up on it!

What do you call skydiving lawyers? Skeet.

What goes clop, clop, clop, bang, bang, clop clop clop? An Amish drive-by shooting.

How are a Texas tornado and a Tennessee divorce the same? Somebody's gonna lose a trailer.

WORD ART.EDU

1. AQUADEXTROUS (ak wa deks' trus) adj. Possessing the ability to turn the bathtub faucet on and off with your toes.

2. CARPERPETUATION (kar' pur pet u a shun) n. The act, when vacuuming, of running over a string or a piece of lint at least a dozen times, reaching over and picking it up, examining it, then putting it back down to give the vacuum one more chance.

3. DISCONFECT (dis kon fekt') v. To sterilize the piece of candy you dropped on the floor by blowing on it, assuming this will somehow 'remove' all the germs.

4. ELBONICS (el bon' iks) n. The actions of two people maneuvering for one armrest in a movie theater (airplane).

5. FRUST (frust) n. The small line of debris that refuses to be swept onto the dust pan and keep backing a person across the room until he finally decides to give up and sweep it under the rug.

6. LACTOMANGULATION (lak' to man guy lay' shun) n. Manhandling the "open here" spout on a milk container so badly that one has to resort to the 'illegal' side.

7. PEPPIER (pehp ee ay') n. The waiter at a fancy restaurant whose sole purpose seems to be walking around asking diners if they want ground pepper.

8. PHONESIA (fo nee' zhuh) n. The affliction of dialing a phone number and forgetting whom you were calling just as they answer.

9. PUPKUS (pup'kus) n. The moist residue left on a window after a dog presses its nose to it.

10. TELECRASTINATION (tel e kras tin ay' shun) n. The act of always letting the phone ring at least twice before you pick it up, even when you're only six inches away.

- NEW WORDS FOR THE NEW MILLENIUM
- BLAMESTORMING: Sitting around in a group, discussing why a deadline was missed or a project failed, and who was responsible.
- CHAINSAW CONSULTANT: An outside expert brought in to reduce the employee headcount, leaving the top brass with clean hands.
- CUBE FARM: An office filled with cubicles.
- IDEA HAMSTERS: People who always seem to have their idea generator running.
- MOUSE POTATO: The on-line, wired generation's answer to the couch potato.
- PRAIRIE DOGGING: When someone yells or drops something loudly in a cube farm, and people's heads pop up over the walls to see what's going on.
- SITCOMs: (Single Income, Two Children, Oppressive Mortgage) What yuppies turn into when they have children and one of them stops working to stay home with the kids.
- STARTER MARRIAGE: A short-lived first marriage that ends in divorce with no kids, no property and no regrets.
- STRESS PUPPY: A person who seems to thrive on being stressed out and whiny.
- SWIPED OUT: An ATM or credit card that has been rendered useless because the magnetic strip is worn away from extensive use.
- TOURISTS: People who take training classes just to get a vacation from their jobs. "We had three serious students in the class; the rest were just tourists."
- TREEWARE: Hacker slang for documentation or other printed material.
- XEROX SUBSIDY: Euphemism for swiping free photocopies from one's workplace.
- ALPHA GEEK: The most knowledgeable, technically proficient person in an office or work group.
- CHIPS & SALSA: Chips = hardware, Salsa = software. "Well, first we gotta figure out if the problem's in your chips or your salsa.

DEFINITIONS BY GENDER.EDU

THINGY:

female: Any part under a car's hood.

male: The strap fastener on a woman's bra.

VULNERABLE:

female: Fully opening up one's self emotionally to another.

male: Playing football without a helmet.

COMMUNICATION:

female: The sharing of thoughts and feelings with one's partner.

male: Leaving a note before suddenly taking off for a weekend with the boys.

BUTT:

female: The body part that "looks bigger" no matter what is worn.

male: What you slap when someone scores a touchdown, home run, or goal. Also good for mooning.

COMMITMENT:

female: A desire to get married and raise a family.

male: Trying not to pick up other women while out with girlfriend.

ENTERTAINMENT:

female: A good movie, concert, play or book.

male: Anything that can be done while drinking

FLATULENCE:

female: An embarrassing by-product of digestion.

male: An endless source of entertainment, self-expression and male bonding.

THOUGHTS TO PONDER.COM

Here are some thoughts to ponder...I hope you find yourself smiling.com

Things to Ponder:

1. I started out with nothing....I still have most of it.
2. When did my wild oats turn to prunes and All Bran?
3. I finally got my head together, now my body is falling apart.
4. Funny, I don't remember being absent minded.
5. All reports are in. Life is now officially unfair.
6. If all is not lost, where is it?
7. It is easier to get older than it is to get wiser.
8. If at first you do succeed, try not to look too astonished.
9. I tried to get a life once, but they were out of stock.
10. I went to school to become a wit, only got halfway through.
11. It was all so different before everything changed.
12. Some days you're the dog, some days you're the hydrant.
13. Nostalgia isn't what it used to be.
14. Old programmers never die. They just terminate and stay resident.
15. I wish the buck stopped here. I could use a few.
16. It's hard to make a comeback when you haven't been anywhere.
17. Living on Earth is expensive, but it does include a free trip around the sun.
18. The only time the world beats a path to your door is if you're in the bathroom.
19. If you're living on the edge, make sure you're wearing your seat belt.
20. There are two kinds of pedestrians...the quick and the dead.
21. A closed mouth gathers no feet.
22. Health is merely the slowest possible rate at which one can die.
23. It's not hard to meet expenses...they're everywhere.

DOOMED TO STUPIDITY.COM

Doomed to Stupidity.com

On Sears hairdryer: Do not use while sleeping. (Gee, that's the only time I have to work on my hair!)

On a bag of Fritos: You could be a winner! No purchase necessary. Details inside. (The shoplifter special!)

On a bar of Dial soap: Directions: Use like regular soap. (and that would be how?)

On some Swann frozen dinners: Serving suggestion: Defrost. (But it's *just* a suggestion!)

On a hotel provided shower cap in a box: Fits one head. (The big one or the little one?)

On Marks & Spencer Bread Pudding: Product will be hot after heating. (Are you sure??? Let's experiment.)

On packaging for a Rowenta iron: Do not iron clothes on body. (But wouldn't that save more time?) (Whose body?)

On Boot's Children's cough medicine: Do not drive car or operate machinery. (We could do a lot to reduce the rate of construction accidents if we just kept 5 year olds off those fork lifts.)

On Nytol sleep aid: Warning: may cause drowsiness. (One would hope!)

On a Korean kitchen knife: Warning keep out of children. (Or pets! What's for dinner?)

On a string of Chinese-made Christmas lights: For indoor or outdoor use only. (As opposed to use in outer space.) (Or underground?)

On a Japanese food processor: Not to be used for the other use. (Now I'm curious.)

On Sainsbury's peanuts: Warning: contains nuts. (And what else?)

On an American Airlines packet of nuts: Instructions: open packet, eat nuts. (Duh!)

On a Swedish chainsaw: Do not attempt to stop chain with your hands or genitals. (What is this, a home castration kit?)

On a child's superman costume: Wearing of this garment does not enable you to fly. (That's right, destroy a universal childhood fantasy!)

These are nominees for the **Chevy Nova Award**, named in Honor of the GM's fiasco in trying to market this car in Central and South America "no va" means, of course, in Spanish, "it doesn't go."

1. The Dairy Association's huge success with the campaign "Got Milk?" prompted them to expand advertising to Mexico. It was soon brought to their attention the Spanish translation read "Are you lactating?"

2. Coors put its slogan, "Turn It Loose," into Spanish, where it was read as "Suffer From Diarrhea."

3. Scandinavian vacuum manufacturer Electrolux used the following in an American campaign: "Nothing sucks like an Electrolux"

4. Clairol introduced the "Mist Stick," a curling iron, into Germany only to find out that "mist" is slang for manure.

5. When Gerber started selling baby food in Africa, they used the same packaging as in the US, with the smiling baby on the label. Later they learned that in Africa, companies routinely put pictures on the labels of what's inside, since many people can't read.

6. Colgate introduced a toothpaste in France called Cue, the name of a notorious porno magazine.

7. An American T-shirt maker in Miami printed shirts for the Spanish market which promoted the Pope's visit. Instead of "I Saw the Pope" (el Papa), the shirts read "I Saw the Potato" (la papa)

8. Pepsi's "Come Alive With the Pepsi Generation" translated into "Pepsi Brings Your Ancestors Back From the Grave" in Chinese.

9. The Coca-Cola name in China was first read as "Kekoukela", meaning "Bite the wax tadpole" or "female horse stuffed with wax",

depending on the dialect. Coke then researched 40,000 characters to find a phonetic equivalent "kokou kole", translating into "happiness in the mouth."

10. Frank Purdue's chicken slogan, "It takes a strong man to make a tender chicken" was translated into Spanish as "it takes an aroused man to make a chicken affectionate"

11. When Parker Pen marketed a ball-point pen in Mexico, its ads were supposed to have read, "It won't leak in your pocket and embarrass you." The company thought that the word "embarazar" (to impregnate) meant to embarrass, so the ad read: "It won't leak in your pocket and make you pregnant!"

12. When American Airlines wanted to advertise its new leather first class seats in the Mexican market, it translated its "Fly In Leather" campaign literally, which meant "Fly Naked" (vuela en cuero) in Spanish.

QUOTES FOR THE SERIOUS.COM

1. A day without sunshine is like—night
2. On the other hand, you have different fingers.
3. 42.7 percent of all statistics are made up on the spot.
4. Save the whales. Collect the whole set.
5. I sometimes feel like I'm diagonally parked in a parallel universe.
6. 99 percent of all lawyers give the rest a bad name.
7. Honk if you love peace and quiet.
8. Remember at least half of all people are below average.
9. Despite the cost of living, have you noticed how popular it remains?
10. Atheism is a non-prophet organization.
11. He who laughs last thinks slowest.
12. Depression is merely anger without enthusiasm.
13. Eagles may soar, but then weasels don't get sucked into jet engines.
14. I drive way too fast to worry about cholesterol.
15. The early bird may get the worm, but the second mouse gets the cheese.
16. Borrow money from a pessimist—they don't expect it back.
17. Quantum mechanics: the dreams stuff is made of.
18. Support bacteria—they're the only culture some people have.
19. When everything's coming your way, you're either in the wrong lane or going the wrong way.
20. A conclusion is the place where you got tired of thinking.
21. Experience is something you don't get until just after you need it.
22. For every action there is an equal and opposite criticism.
23. Bills travel through the mail at twice the speed of checks
24. Never do card tricks for the group you play poker with.
25. No one is listening until you make a mistake.
26. Success always occurs in private and failure in full view.

27. The hardness of butter is directly proportional to the softness of the bread.
28. The severity of the itch is inversely proportional to the ability to reach it.
29. To steal ideas from one person is plagiarism; to steal from many is research.
30. To succeed in politics, it is often necessary to rise above your principles.
31. You never really learn to swear until you learn to drive.
32. The problem with the gene pool is that there is no lifeguard.
33. The sooner you fall behind the more time you'll have to catch up.
34. A clear conscience is usually the sign of a bad memory.
35. Change is inevitable except from vending machines.
36. Plan to be spontaneous—tomorrow.
37. Always try to be modest and be proud of it!
38. If you think nobody cares about you, try missing a couple of payments.
39. How many of you believe in telekinesis? Raise my hand…
40. If at first you don't succeed, then skydiving isn't for you.

FOR WOMEN ONLY.COM

1. Don't imagine you can change a man—unless he's in diapers.
2. What do you do if your boyfriend walks-out? You shut the door.
3. If they put a man on the moon—they should be able to put them all up there.
4. Never let your man's mind wander—it's too little to be out alone.
5. Go for younger men. You might as well—they never mature anyway.
6. Men are all the same—they just have different faces, so that you can tell them apart.
7. Definition of a bachelor; a man who has missed the opportunity to make some woman miserable.
8. Women don't make fools of men—most of them are the do-it-yourself types.
9. Best way to get a man to do something, is to suggest they are too old for it.
10. Love is blind, but marriage is a real eye-opener.
11. If you want a committed man, look in a mental hospital.
12. The children of Israel wandered around the desert for 40 years. Even in biblical times, men wouldn't ask for directions.
13. If he asks what sort of books you're interested in, tell him checkbooks.
14. Remember a sense of humor does not mean that you tell him jokes, it means that you laugh at his.
15. Sadly, all men are created equal.

EXPRESSIONS FOR A WOMAN'S HIGH STRESS DAYS.com
1. Well, this day was a total waste of makeup.
2. Not the brightest crayon in the box now, are we?
3. You! Off my planet !!

4. Errors have been made. Others will be blamed.
5. ...would be...?
6. I'm not crazy, I've just been in a very bad mood for 30 years.
7. Allow me to introduce my selves.
8. Sarcasm is just one more service we offer.
9. Whatever kind of look you were going for, you missed.
10. Do they ever shut up on your planet?
11. I'm just working here till a good fast-food job opens up.
12. I'm trying to imagine you with a personality.
13. Stress is when you wake up screaming & you realize you haven't fallen asleep yet.
14. I can't remember if I'm the good twin or the evil one.
15. How many times do I have to flush before you go away?
16. I have a computer, a vibrator, & pizza delivery. Why should I leave the house?
17. I just want revenge. Is that so wrong?
18. You say I'm a bitch like it's a bad thing.
19. Can I trade this job for what's behind door #2?
20. Okay, okay, I take it back! UnF—k you!
21. Nice perfume. Must you marinate in it?
22. Chaos, panic, & disorder—my work here is done.
23. Everyone thinks I'm psychotic, except for my friends deep inside the earth.
24. Earth is full. Go home.
25. Is it time for your medication or mine?
26. Aw, did I step on your poor little bitty ego?
27. How do I set a laser printer to stun?
28. I'm not tense, just terribly, terribly alert.
29. When I want your opinion, I'll give it to you.

1. I'm out of estrogen—I have a gun
2. Guys have feelings too. But like…who cares?
3. I don't believe in miracles. I rely on them.
4. Next mood swing: 6 minutes.
5. And your point is…
6. I used to be schizophrenic, but we're OK now.
7. I'm busy. You're ugly. Have a nice day.
8. Warning: I have an attitude and I know how to use it.
9. Of course I don't look busy…I did it right the first time.
10. Why do people with closed minds always open their mouths?
11. I'm multi-talented: I can talk and annoy you at the same time.
12. Do NOT start with me. You will NOT win.
13. You have the right to remain silent, so please SHUT UP.
14. All stressed out and no one to choke.
15. I'm one of those bad things that happen to good people.
16. How can I miss you if you won't go away?
17. Sorry if I looked interested. I'm not.
18. Objects Under This Shirt Are Larger Than They Appear.

TESTS.EDU

THIS IS JUST A TEST.edu

1. Who's that playing the piano on the "Mad About You" theme?
2. What occurs more often in December than any other month?
3. Only 14% of Americans say they've done this with the opposite sex. What is it?
4. What separates "60 Minutes," on CBS, from every other TV show?
5. Half of all Americans live within 50 miles of what?
6. Most boat owners name their boats. What is the most popular boat name requested?
7. More women do this in the bathroom than men.
8. What do 100% of all lottery winners do?
9. In a recent survey, Americans revealed that this was their favorite smell.
10. If you were to spell out numbers, how far would you have to go until you would find the letter "A"?
11. What do bullet proof vests, fire escapes, windshield wipers and laser printers all have in common?
12. Married men revealed that they do this twice as often as single men.
13. This stimulates 29 muscles and chemicals causing relaxation. Women seem to like it light and frequent, men like it more strenuous.
14. This is the only food that doesn't spoil.
15. There are more collect calls on this day than any other day of the year.
16. What trivia fact about Mel Blanc (voice of Bugs Bunny) is most ironic?
17. 40% of all people who come to a party in your home do this?
18. 3.9% of all women surveyed say they never do this.
19. What common everyday occurrence is composed of 59% nitrogen, 21% hydrogen and 9% dioxide?

20. About 1/3 of all Americans say they do this while sitting?
21. What person, not a "Seinfeld" regular cast member, is featured on every episode of "Seinfeld"?

THESE ARE JUST THE ANSWERS.*edu*

1. Paul Reiser, himself.
2. Conception.
3. Skinny dipping.
4. No theme song/music.
5. Their birthplace. This is propinquity.
6. Obsession
7. Wash their hands. Women~80% Men~55%
8. Gain weight
9. Banana.
10. One thousand
11. All invented by women.
12. Change their underwear.
13. A kiss
14. Honey
15. Father's Day
16. He was allergic to carrots.
17. Snoop in your medicine cabinet.
18. Wear underwear
19. A fart.
20. Flush the toilet.
21. Superman, either by name or pictures on Jerry's refrigerator.

How many do you remember.*edu*

1. Blackjack chewing gum
2. Wax Coke-shaped bottles with colored sugar water
3. Candy cigarettes
4. Soda pop machines that dispensed bottles
5. Hamburg joints with tableside jukeboxes

6. Home milk delivery in glass bottles with cardboard stoppers

7. Party lines

8. Newsreels before the movie

9. Slingshots

10. Butch wax

11. Telephone numbers with a word prefix (Olive—6933)

12. Peashooters

13. Howdy Doody

14. 45 RPM records

15. S&H Green Stamps

16. Hi-fi's

17. Metal ice trays with levers

18. Mimeograph paper

19. Blue flashbulbs

20. Amos and Andy

21. Roller skate keys

22. Cork popguns

23. Drive-ins

24. Studebakers

25. Wash tub wringers

If you remembered 0–5=You're still young

If you remembered 6–10=You are getting older

If you remembered 11–15=Don't tell your age

If you remembered 16–25=You're older than dirt!

 NOSTALGIA TEST.edu

ANSWERS TO FOLLOW

1. "Kookie; Kookie. Lend me your_____."

2. The "battle cry" of the hippies in the sixties was "Turn on; tune in;_____."

3. After the Lone Ranger saved the day and rode off into the sunset, the grateful citizens would ask, "Who was that masked man?" Invariably, someone would answer, "I don't know, but he left this behind." What did he leave behind_____?

4. Folk songs were played side by side with rock and roll. One of the most memorable folk songs included these lyrics: "When the rooster crows at the break of dawn, look out your window and I'll be gone. You're the reason I'm traveling on_____."

5. A group of protesters arrested at the Democratic convention in Chicago in 1968 achieved cult status, and were known as the_____.

6. When the Beatles first came to the U.S. in early 1964, we all watched them on the _____show.

7. Some of us who protested the Vietnam war did so by burning our_____.

8. We all learned to read using the same books. We read about the thrilling lives and adventures of Dick and Jane. What was the name of Dick and Jane's dog?_____.

9. The cute, little car with the engine in the back and the trunk (what there was of it) in the front, was called the VW. What other name(s) did it go by?_____ & _____

10. A Broadway musical and movie gave us the gang names the _____and the_____.

11. In the seventies, we called the drop-out nonconformists "hippies." But in the early sixties, they were known as_____.

12. William Bendix played Chester A. Riley, who always seemed to get the short end of the stick in the television program, "The Life of Riley." At the end of each show, poor Chester would turn to the camera and exclaim, "What a_____."

13. "Get your kicks,_____."

14. "The story you are about to see is true. The names have been changed_____."

15. The real James Bond, Sean Connery, mixed his martinis a special way:_____.

16. "In the jungle, the mighty jungle,_____."

17. That "adult" book by Henry Miller—the one that contained all the "dirty" dialogue—was called _____.

18. Today, the math geniuses in school might walk around with a calculator strapped to their belt. But back in the sixties, members of the math club used a _____.

19. In 1971, singer Don Maclean sang a song about "the day the music died." This was a reference and tribute to _____.

20. A well-known television commercial featured a driver who was miraculously lifted through thin air and into the front seat of a convertible. The matching slogan was "Let Hertz _____."

21. After the twist, the mashed potatoes, and the watusi, we "danced" under a stick that was lowered as low as we could go in a dance called the_____.

22. "N-E-S-T-L-E-S; Nestles makes the very best…_____."

23. In the late sixties, the "full figure" style of Jane Russell and Marilyn Monroe gave way to the "trim" look, as first exemplified by British model _____.

24. Sachmo was America's "ambassador of goodwill." Our parents shared this great jazz trumpet player with us. His name was

_____.

25. On Jackie Gleason's variety show in the sixties, one of the most popular segments was "Joe, the Bartender." Joe's regular visitor at the bar was that slightly off- center, but lovable character, _____. (The character's name, not the actor's.)

26. We can remember the first satellite placed into orbit. The Russians did it; it was called _____.

27. What takes a licking and keeps on ticking?_____.

28. One of the big fads of the late fifties and sixties was a large plastic ring that we twirled around our waist; it was called the _____.
29. The "Age of Aquarius" was brought into the mainstream in the Broadway musical _____.
30. This is a two-parter: Red Skelton's hobo character (not the hayseed; the hobo) was_____. Red ended his television show by saying, "Good night, and_____."

THE ANSWERS:
1. "Kookie; Kookie; lend me your comb." If you said "ears," you're in the wrong millennium, pal; you've spent way too much time in Latin class.
2. The "battle cry"" of the hippies in the sixties was "Turn on; tune in; drop out." Many people who proclaimed that 30 years ago today are Wall Street bond traders and corporate lawyers.
3. The Lone Ranger left behind a silver bullet. Several of you said he left behind his mask. Oh, no; even off the screen, Clayton Moore would not be seen as the Lone Ranger without his mask!
4. "When the rooster crows at the break of dawn, look out your window and I'll be gone. You're the reason I'm traveling on; Don't think twice, it's all right."
5. The group of protesters arrested at the Democratic convention in Chicago in 1968 were known as the Chicago seven. As Paul Harvey says, "They would like me to mention their names."
6. When the Beatles first came to the U.S. in early 1964, we all watched them on the Ed Sullivan Show.
7. Some of us who protested the Vietnam war did so by burning our draft cards. If you said "bras," you've got the right spirit, but nobody ever burned a bra while I was watching. The "bra burning" days came as a by-product of women's liberation movement, which had nothing directly to do with the Viet Nam war.

8. Dick and Jane's dog was Spot. "See Spot run." Whatever happened to them? Rumor has it they have been replaced in some school systems by "Heather Has Two Mommies."
9. It was the VW Beetle, or more affectionately, the Bug.
10. A Broadway musical and movie gave us the gang names the Sharks and the Jets. West Side Story.
11. In the early sixties, the drop-out, non-conformists were known as beatniks. Maynard G. Krebs was the classic beatnik, except that he had no rhythm, man; a beard, but no beat.
12. At the end of "The Life of Riley," Chester would turn to the camera and exclaim, "What a revolting development this is."
13. "Get your kicks, on Route 66."
14. "The story you are about to see is true. The names have been changed to protect the innocent."
15. The real James Bond, Sean Connery, mixed his martinis a special way: shaken, not stirred.
16. "In the jungle, the mighty jungle, the lion sleeps tonight."
17. That "adult" book by Henry Miller was called Tropic of Cancer. Today, it would hardly rate a PG-13 rating.
18. Back in the sixties, members of the math club used a slide rule.
19. "The day the music died" was a reference and tribute to Buddy Holly.
20. The matching slogan was "Let Hertz put you in the driver's seat."
21. After the twist, the mashed potatoes, and the watusi, we "danced" under a stick in a dance called the Limbo.
22. "N-E-S-T-L-E-S; Nestles makes the very best chooo-c'late." In the television commercial, "chocolate" was sung by a puppet—a dog. (Remember his mouth flopping open and shut?)
23. In the late sixties, the "full figure" style gave way to the "trim" look, as first exemplified by British model Twiggy.
24. Our parents shared this great jazz trumpet player with us. His name was Louis Armstrong.
25. Joe's regular visitor at the bar was Crazy Googenhiem.

26. The Russians put the first satellite into orbit; it was called Sputnik.
27. What takes a licking and keeps on ticking? A Timex watch.
28. The large plastic ring that we twirled around our waist was called the hula-hoop.
29. The "Age of Aquarius" was brought into the mainstream in the Broadway musical "Hair."
30. Red Skelton's hobo character was Freddie the Freeloader. (Clem Kaddiddlehopper was the "hay seed.") Red ended his television show by saying, "Good night, and may God bless." ,

CLASSIC LATERAL THINKING EXERCISES.edu

These are great. Get your thinking cap on! Try these to loosen up the old brain cells....

1. There is a man who lives on the top floor of a very tall building. Everyday he gets the elevator down to the ground floor to leave the building to go to work. Upon returning from work though, he can only travel half way up in the lift and has to walk the rest of the way unless it's raining! Why?

This is probably the best known and most celebrated of all lateral thinking puzzles. It is a true classic. Although there are many possible solutions which fit the initial conditions, only the canonical answer is truly satisfying.

2. A man and his son are in a car accident. The father dies on the scene, but the child is rushed to the hospital. When he arrives the surgeon says, "I can't operate on this boy, he is my son!" How can this be?
3. A man is wearing black. Black shoes, socks, trousers, jumper, gloves and balaclava. He is walking down a black street with all the street lamps off. A black car is coming towards him with its lights off but somehow manages to stop in time. How did the driver see the man?
4. One day Kerry celebrated her birthday. Two days later her older twin brother, Terry, celebrated his birthday. How?

5. Why is it better to have round manhole covers than square ones? This is logical rather than lateral, but it is a good puzzle that can be solved by lateral thinking techniques. It is supposedly used by a very well-known software company as an interview question for prospective employees.

6. A man went to a party and drank some of the punch. He then left early. Everyone else at the party who drank the punch subsequently died of poisoning. Why did the man not die?

7. A man died and went to Heaven. There were thousands of other people there. They were all naked and all looked as they did at the age of 21. He looked around to see if there was anyone he recognized. He saw a couple and he knew immediately that they were Adam and Eve. How did he know?

8. A woman had two sons who were born on the same hour of the same day of the same year. But they were not twins. How could this be so?

9. A man walks into a bar and asks the barman for a glass of water. The barman pulls out a gun and points it at the man. The man says 'Thank you' and walks out.

This puzzle claims to be the best of the genre. It is simple in its statement, absolutely baffling and yet with a completely satisfying solution. Most people struggle very hard to solve this one yet they like the answer when they hear it or have the satisfaction of figuring it out.

Answers to follow.

Lateral Thinking Exercises…SOLUTIONS.edu

1. The man is very, very short and can only reach halfway up the elevator buttons. However, if it is raining then he will have his umbrella with him and can press the higher buttons with it.

2. The surgeon was his mother.

3. It was day time.

4. At the time she went into labor, the mother of the twins was traveling by boat. The older twin, Terry, was born first early on March 1st. The

boat then crossed a time zone and Kerry, the younger twin, was born on February the 28th. Therefore, the younger twin celebrates her birthday two days before her older brother.

5. A square manhole cover can be turned and dropped down the diagonal of the manhole. A round manhole cannot be dropped down the manhole. So for safety and practicality, all manhole covers should be round.

6. The poison in the punch came from the ice cubes. When the man drank the punch, the ice was fully frozen. Gradually it melted, poisoning the punch.

7. He recognized Adam and Eve as the only people without navels. Because they were not born of women, they had never had umbilical cords and therefore they never had navels. This one seems perfectly logical but it can sometimes spark fierce theological arguments.

8. They were two of a set of triplets (or quadruplets, etc.). This puzzle stumps many people. They try outlandish solutions involving test-tube babies or surrogate mothers. Why does the brain search for complex solutions when there is a much simpler one available?

9. The man had hiccups. The barman recognized this from his speech and drew the gun in order to give him a shock. It worked and cured the hiccups—so the man no longer needed the water. This is a simple puzzle to state but a difficult one to solve. It is a perfect example of a seemingly irrational and incongruous situation having a simple and complete explanation.

You've got personality.edu

Grab a pencil and paper and keep track of your letter answers. There are 10 questions. Make sure you change the subject of the Email to your total. When you're finished, forward this to everyone you know and the person who sent it to you. Make sure you put your score in as the subject also.

1. When do you feel your best?
   (a) In the morning

(b) During the afternoon and early evening

(c) Late at night

2. You usually walk

(a) fairly fast, with long steps

(b) fairly fast, but with short, quick steps

(c) less fast, head up, looking the world in the face

(d) less fast, head down

(e) very slowly

3. When talking to people, you

(a) stand with your arms folded

(b) have your hands clasped

(c) have one or both your hands on your hips

(d) touch or push the person to whom you are talking

(e) play with your ear, touch your chin, or smooth your hair

4. When relaxing, you sit with

(a) your knees bent and your legs neatly side by side

(b) your legs crossed

(c) your legs stretched out or straight

(d) with one leg curled under you

5. When something really amuses you, you react with

(a) a big, appreciative laugh

(b) a laugh, but not a loud one

(c) a quiet chuckle

(e) a sheepish smile

6. When you go to a party or social gathering, you

(a) make a loud entrance so everyone notices you

(b) make a quiet entrance, looking around for someone you know

(c) make quietest possible entrance and try to stay unnoticed

7 You are working hard, concentrating hard. You are interrupted. You:

(a) welcome the break

(b) feel extremely irritated

(c) vary between these two extremes

8. Which of the following colors do you like most?
   (a) red or orange
   (b) black
   (c) yellow or light blue
   (d) green
   (e) dark blue or purple
   (f) white
   (g) brown or gray
9. When you are in bed at night, in those last few moments before going to sleep, you lie
   (a) stretched out on your back
   (b) stretched out face down on your stomach
   (c) on your side, slightly curled
   (d) with your head on one arm
   (e) with your head under the covers
10. You often dream that you are
    (a) falling
    (b) fighting or struggling
    (c) searching for something or somebody
    (d) flying or floating
    (e) You usually have a dreamless sleep
    (f) Your dreams are always pleasant

POINTS:

1.	(a) 2	(b) 4	(c) 6		
2.	(a) 6	(b) 4	(c) 7	(d) 2	(e) 1
3.	(a) 4	(b) 2	(c) 5	(d) 7	(e) 6
4.	(a) 4	(b) 6	(c) 2	(d) 1	
5.	(a) 6	(b) 4	(c) 3	(d) 5	(e) 2
6.	(a) 6	(b) 4	(c) 2		
7.	(a) 6	(b) 2	(c) 4		

8. (a) 6   (b) 7   (c) 5   (d) 4   (e) 3   (f) 2
    (g) 1
9. (a) 7   (b) 6   (c) 4   (d) 2   (e) 1
10. (a) 4   (b) 2   (c) 3   (d) 5   (e) 6   (f) 1

Add the total number of points.

OVER 60 POINTS: Others see you as someone they should "handle with care." You are seen as vain, self-centered, and extremely dominant. Others may admire you and wish they could be more like you, but they don't always trust you and hesitate to become too deeply involved with you.

FROM 51 TO 60 POINTS: Your friends see you as an exciting, highly volatile, rather impulsive personality; a natural leader, quick to make decisions (though not always the right ones). They see you as bold and venturesome, someone who will try anything once; someone who takes a chance and enjoys an adventure. They enjoy being in your company because of the excitement you radiate.

FROM 41 TO 50 POINTS: Others see you as fresh, lively, charming, amusing, practical, and always interesting; someone who is constantly the center of attention, but sufficiently well-balanced not to let it go to your head. They see you also as kind, considerate, and understanding; someone who will cheer them up and help them out.

FROM 31 TO 40 POINTS: Other people see you as sensible, cautious, careful, and practical. They see you as clever, gifted, or talented, but modest. Not a person who makes friends too quickly or too easily, but someone who is extremely loyal to the friends you do make and who expects the same loyalty in return. Those who really get to know you realize that it takes a lot to shake your trust in your friends, but, equally, that it takes you a long time to get over it if that trust is broken.

FROM 21 TO 30 POINTS: Your friends see you as painstaking and fussy. They see you as very, very cautious and extremely careful, a slow and steady plodder. It would really surprise them if you ever did something impulsively or on the spur of the moment. They expect you to examine everything carefully from every side and then, usually, decide against it.

They think this reaction on your part is caused partly by your careful nature and partly by laziness.

UNDER 21 POINTS: People think you are shy, nervous, and indecisive, someone who needs to be looked after, who always wants someone else to make the decisions and who doesn't want to get involved with anyone or anything. They see you as a worrier, who sees problems that don't exist. Some people think you're boring. Only the people who know you well know that you aren't.

Now, forward this to everyone you know—make sure you put your score in as the subject. yeah right!!!! clog up the whole internet with trivia.

TEACHING STORIES.EDU

The Most Caring Child

Author and lecturer Leo Buscaglia once talked about a contest he was asked to judge. The purpose of the contest was to find the most caring child. The winner was a four year old child whose next door neighbor was an elderly gentleman who had recently lost his wife. Upon seeing the man cry, the little boy went into the old gentleman's yard, climbed onto his lap, and just sat there. When his mother asked him what he had said to the neighbor, the little boy said, "Nothing, I just helped him cry."

What It Means to Be Adopted

Teacher Debbie Moon's first graders were discussing a picture of a family. One little boy in the picture had a different color hair than the other family members. One child suggested that he was adopted and a little girl said, "I know all about adoptions because I was adopted." "What does it mean to be adopted?" asked another child. "It means," said the girl, "that you grew in your mommy's heart instead of her tummy."

Barney

A four year old was at the pediatrician for a check up. As the doctor looked down her ears with an osteoscope, he asked, "Do you think I'll find Big Bird in here?" The little girl stayed silent. Next, the doctor took a tongue depressor and looked down her throat. He asked, "Do you think I'll find the Cookie Monster down there?" Again, the little girl was silent. Then the doctor put a stethoscope to her chest. As he listened to her heart beat, he asked, "Do you think I'll hear Barney in there?" "Oh, no!" the little girl replied. "Jesus is in my heart. Barney's on my underpants."

Discouraged?

As I was driving home from work one day, I stopped to watch a local Little League baseball game that was being played in a park near my home. As I sat down behind the bench on the first-base line, I asked one of the boys what the score was. "We're behind 14 to nothing," he answered with a smile. "Really," I said. "I have to say you don't look very discouraged." "Discouraged?" the boy asked with a puzzled look on his face. "Why should we be discouraged? We haven't been up to bat yet."

Roles And How We Play Them

Whenever I'm disappointed with my spot in my life, I stop and think about little Jamie Scott. Jamie was trying out for a part in a school play. His mother told me that he'd set his heart on being in it, though she feared he would not be chosen. On the day the parts were awarded, I went with her to collect him after school. Jamie rushed up to her, eyes shining with pride and excitement. "Guess what Mom," he shouted, and then said those words that will remain a lesson to me: "I've been chosen to clap and cheer."

A Lesson In Heart

A lesson in "heart" is my little, 10 year old daughter, Sarah, who was born with a muscle missing in her foot and wears a brace all the time. She came home one beautiful spring day to tell me she had competed in "field day"—that's where they have lots of races and other competitive events. Because of her leg support, my mind raced as I tried to think of encouragement for my Sarah, things I could say to her about not letting

this get her down—but before I could get a word out, she said "Daddy, I won two of the races!" I couldn't believe it! And then Sarah said, "I had an advantage." Ah. I knew it. I thought she must have been given a head start…some kind of physical advantage. But again, before I could say anything, she said, "Daddy, I didn't get a head start…My advantage was I had to try harder!"

The Shoes

A little boy about 10 years old was standing before a shoe store on the roadway, barefooted, peering through the window, and shivering with cold. A lady approached the boy and said, "My little fellow, why are you looking earnestly in that window?" "I was asking God to give me a pair of shoes," was the boys reply. The lady took him by the hand and went into the store and asked the clerk to get half a dozen pairs of socks for the boy. She then asked if he could give her a basin of water and a towel He quickly brought them to her. She took the little fellow to the back part of the store and, removing her gloves, knelt down, washed his little feet, and dried them with a towel. By this time the store owner was back with a pair of shoes. Placing a pair upon the boy's feet, she purchased him a pair of shoes. She tied up the remaining pairs of socks and gave them to him. She patted him on the head and said, "No doubt, my little fellow, you feel more comfortable now?" As she turned to go, the astonished lad caught her by the hand, and looking up in her face, with tears in his eyes, answered the question with these words: "Are you God's Wife?"

ETHICS.EDU

TWO ETHICAL QUESTIONS and ONE TO PROVOKE THOUGHT

Q1: If you knew a woman who was pregnant, who had 8 kids already, three who were deaf, two who were blind, one mentally retarded, and she had syphilis; would you recommend that she have an abortion?

Read the next question before scrolling down to the answer of this one or turning the page in this case.

Q2: It is time to elect the world leader, and your vote counts. Here are the facts about the three leading candidates:

Candidate A

Associates with crooked politicians, and consults with astrologists. He's had two mistresses. He also chain smokes and drinks 8 to 10 martinis a day.

Candidate B

He was kicked out of office twice, sleeps until noon, used opium in college and drinks a quart of whisky every evening.

Candidate C

He is a decorated war hero. He's a vegetarian, doesn't smoke, drinks an occasional beer and hasn't had any extramarital affairs.

Which of these candidates would be your choice? A, B, C.

Q3: Would you buy stock in the following company?

29 have been accused of spousal abuse

7 have been arrested for fraud

19 have been accused of writing bad checks

* 117 have bankrupted at least two businesses

3 have been arrested for assault

71 cannot get a credit card due to bad credit

14 have been arrested on drug-related charges

8 have been arrested for shoplifting

21 are current defendants in lawsuits

In 1998 alone, 84 were stopped for drunk driving

Can you guess which organization this is?

Decide first, no peeking, then scroll down for the answer

or in this case turn the page.

Q1:

Candidate A is Franklin D. Roosevelt

Candidate B is Winston Churchill

Candidate C is Adolph Hitler

…and by the way:

Answer to the abortion question Q2:—if you said yes, you just killed Beethoven.

and with your tax dollars…

Q3: It's the 535 members of your United States Congress.gov

The same group that perpetually cranks out hundreds upon hundreds of new laws designed to keep the rest of us in line.

On that note Effective immediately

I am hereby officially tendering my resignation as an adult. I have decided I would like to accept the responsibilities of an 8 year old again. I want to go to McDonald's and think that it's a four star restaurant. I want to sail sticks across a fresh mud puddle and make ripples with rocks. I want to think M&Ms are better than money because you can eat them. I want to lie under a big oak tree and run a lemonade stand with my friends on a hot summer's day.

I want to return to a time when life was simple. When all you knew were colors, multiplication tables, and nursery rhymes, but that didn't bother you, because you didn't know what you didn't know and you didn't care. All you knew was to be happy because you were blissfully unaware of all the things that should make you worried or upset. I want to believe that anything is possible. I want to be oblivious to the complexities of life and be overly excited by the little things again. I want to live simple again.

I don't want my day to consist of computer crashes, mountains of paperwork, depressing news, how to survive more days in the month than there is money in the bank, doctor bills, gossip, illness, and loss of loved ones. I want to believe in the power of smiles, hugs, a kind word, truth, justice, peace, dreams, the imagination, mankind, and making angels in the snow.

So….here's my checkbook and my car-keys, my credit card bills and my 401K statements. I am officially resigning from adulthood. And if you want to discuss this further, you'll have to catch me first, cause…"Tag! You're it!"

MOTHERS.COM

Real Mothers.com

Real Mothers don't eat quiche; they don't have time to make it.

Real Mothers know that their kitchen utensils are probably in the sandbox.

Real Mothers often have sticky floors, filthy ovens and happy kids.

Real Mothers know that dried playdough doesn't come out of shag carpet.

Real Mothers don't want to know what the vacuum just sucked up.

Real Mothers sometimes ask "why me?" and get their answer when a little voice says, "because I love you best."

Real Mothers know that a child's growth is not measured by height or years or grade…It is marked by the progression of Mama to Mommy to Mom….

THINGS ONLY A MOM CAN TEACH

1. My Mother taught me about ANTICIPATION…"Just wait until your father gets home."

2. My Mother taught me about RECEIVING…"You are going to get it when we get home!"

3. My Mother taught me to MEET A CHALLENGE…"What were you thinking? Answer me when I talk to you…Don't talk back to me!"

4. My Mother taught me LOGIC…"If you fall out off that swing and break your neck, you're not going to the store with me."

5. My Mother taught me MEDICAL SCIENCE…"If you don't stop crossing your eyes, they are going to freeze that way."

6. My Mother taught me to THINK AHEAD…"If you don't pass your spelling test, you'll never get a good job."

7. My Mother taught me ESP…"Put your sweater on; don't you think I know when you're cold?"
8. My Mother taught me HUMOR…"When that lawn mower cuts off your toes, don't come running to me."
9. My Mother taught me how to BECOME AN ADULT…"If you don't eat your vegetables, you'll never grow up."
10. My Mother taught me about SEX…"How do you think you got here?"
11. My Mother taught me about GENETICS…"You're just like your father."
12. My Mother taught me about my ROOTS…"Do you think you were born in a barn?"
13. My Mother taught me about WISDOM OF AGE…"When you get to be my age, you will understand."
14. And my all time favorite…JUSTICE…"One day you'll have kids of your own and I hope they turn out just like you…Then you'll see what it's like."

The Real Images of Mother:
4 YEARS OF AGE
My Mommy can do anything!
8 YEARS OF AGE
My Mom knows a lot! A whole lot!
12 YEARS OF AGE
My Mother doesn't really know quite everything.
14 YEARS OF AGE
Naturally, Mother doesn't know that, either.
16 YEARS OF AGE
Mother? She's hopelessly old-fashioned
18 YEARS OF AGE
That old woman? She's way out of date!
25 YEARS OF AGE
Well, she might know a little bit about it.

35 YEARS OF AGE
Before we decide, let's get Mom's opinion.
45 YEARS OF AGE
Wonder what Mom would have thought about it?
65 YEARS OF AGE
Wish I could talk it over with Mom....

No Charge

My little boy came into the kitchen this evening while I was fixing supper. And he handed me a piece of paper he'd been writing on. So, after wiping my hands on my apron, I read it,
and this is what it said:
For mowing the grass, $5.
For making my own bed this week, $1.
For going to the store $.50.
For playing with baby brother while you went shopping, $.25.
For taking out the trash, $1.
For getting a good report card, $5.
And for raking the yard, $2.
Well, I looked at him standing there expectantly, and a thousand memories flashed through my mind. So, I picked up the paper, and turning it over, this is what I wrote:
For the nine months I carried you, growing inside me, No Charge.
For the nights I sat up with you, doctored you, prayed for you, No charge.
For the time and the tears, and the cost through the years, No Charge.
For the nights filled with dread, and the worries ahead, No Charge.
For advice and the knowledge, and the cost of your college, No Charge.
For the toys, food and clothes, and for wiping your nose, No Charge.
Son, when you add it all up, the full cost of my love is No Charge.
Well, when he finished reading, he had great big tears in his eyes. And he looked up at me and he said, "Mama, I sure do love you." Then he took the pen and in great big letters he wrote: PAID IN FULL.

A CHILD'S BILL OF RIGHTS.edu
Author Unknown
My son came home from school one day,
With that smile on his face.
Watch me blow my Mom away,
I'll put her in her place.
Guess what I learned in Civics Two,
Taught by Mr. Wright.
It was all about the law today,

THE CHILDREN'S BILL OF RIGHTS.
I don't have to clean my room or
Even cut my hair.
No one can tell me what to eat
Or choose the clothes I wear.
Freedom of speech is my
Constitutional guarantee.
It is my choice of what to read
Or watch on the T.V.
I have the freedom of religion,
And no matter what you say,
I don't have to ask your God for help,
I don't have to kneel to pray.
I can also wear an earring in my ear
Or even pierce my nose.
I can have the Devil's number
Tattooed across my toes.
Hey, if you ever spank me,
I can charge you with assault.
I can back up all my charges
With the black and blue results.
Don't ever touch my body,

It is for me to use,
For all those hugs and kisses
Are a form of sex abuse.
Don't fill my head with morals
Like your mother did to you.
There's such a thing called mind Control,
that is illegal too.
Mom, I have these children's rights.
You can't do a thing to me.
I'll just call the children's services,
Better known as C.S.D.
My very first impression was
To toss him out the door,
But here is a chance to teach a lesson
For once and ever more.
I kind of mulled it over,
But I didn't let it go.
This kid of mine doesn't realize,
He is working with a pro.
The next day I took him shopping.
Much to his dismay,
I didn't buy him 501's
Or shirts designed by Nike.
I called and talked to C.S.D.
They said they didn't care,
If I bought him Volume shoes,
Or a pair of Nike Airs.
I canceled out his appointment
To test his driving SKILLS.
I'd probably be dead by now,
If only looks could kill.
I don't have time to stop and eat,

Get stuff for you to munch.
I followed C.S.D.'s advice,
I bought you a big sack lunch.
So, you say you're not so hungry,
You can wait till dinner time.
I am fixing liver and onions,
A favorite dish of mine.
So, you want to get a movie
To watch on the V.C.R.
Gosh! I sold that television
To buy tires for my car.
I also rented out your room,
You don't really need a bed.
All I really have to do
Is put a roof over your head.
As long as I will buy your clothes
And all the food you eat,
I can keep your allowance
And buy me something really neat.
I know you like the tacos after
We have shopped all day.
Son, I have my bill of rights,
They go in effect today.
Son, why are you crying?
What are you doing on your knees?
You're asking God to help you,
Instead of C.S.D.?

WHEN GOD MADE MOMS

By the time the Lord made mothers, he was into his sixth day of working overtime. An Angel appeared and said "Why are you spending so much time on this one"? And the Lord answered and said, "Have you seen the spec sheet on her? She has to be completely washable, but not plastic, have 200 movable parts, all replaceable, run on black coffee and leftovers, have a lap that can hold three children at one time and that disappears when she stands up, have a kiss that can cure anything from a scraped knee to a broken heart, and have six pairs of hands." The Angel was astounded at the requirements for this one. "Six pairs of hands! No Way!" said the Angel. The Lord replied, "Oh, it's not the hands that are the problem. It's the three pairs of eyes that mothers must have!" "And that's just on the standard model?" the Angel asked.

The Lord nodded in agreement, "Yep, one pair of eyes are to see through the closed door as she asks her children what they are doing even though she already knows. Another pair in the back of her head, are to see what she needs to know even though no one thinks she can. And the third pair are here in the front of her head. They are for looking at an errant child and saying that she understands and loves him or her without even a single word."

The Angel tried to stop the Lord. "This is too much work for one day. Wait until tomorrow to finish." "But I can't!" The Lord protested, "I am so close to finishing this creation that is so close to my own heart. She already heals herself when she is sick AND can feed a family of six on a pound of hamburger and can get a nine year old to stand in the shower." The Angel moved closer and touched the woman, "But you have made her so soft, Lord." "She is soft," the Lord agreed, "but I have also made her tough. You have no idea what she can endure or accomplish." "Will she be able to think?" asked the Angel. The Lord replied, "Not only will she be able to think, she will be able to reason, and negotiate."

The Angel then noticed something and reached out and touched the woman's cheek. "Oops, it looks like you have a leak with this model. I told you that you were trying to put too much into this one." " That's not a leak," the Lord objected. "That's a tear!" " "What's the tear for?" the Angel asked. The Lord said, "The tear is her way of expressing her joy, her sorrow, her disappointment, her pain, her loneliness, her grief, and her pride." The Angel was impressed. "You are a genius, Lord. You thought of everything, Mothers are truly amazing."

YOUR NAME.COM

According to studies, the first letter of your first name reveals your sexual identity.edu

-A-

You are not particularly romantic, but you are interested in action. You mean business. With you, what you see is what you get. You have no patience for flirting and can't be bothered with someone who is trying to be coy, cute, demure, and subtly enticing. You are an up front person. When it comes to sex, it's action that counts not obscure hints. Your mate's physical attractiveness is important to you. You find the chase and challenge of the "hunt" invigorating. You are passionate and sexual as well as being much more adventurous than you appear; however, you do not go around advertising these qualities. Your physical needs are your primary concern.

-B-

You give off vibes of lazy sensuality. You enjoy being romanced, wined, and dined. You are very happy to receive gifts as an expression of the affection of your lover. You want to be pampered and know how to pamper your mate. You are private in your expression of endearments and particularly when it comes to lovemaking. You will hold off until everything meets with your approval. You can control your appetite and abstain from sex if need be. You require new sensations and experiences. You are willing to experiment.

-C-

You are a very social individual, and it is important to you to have a relationship. You require closeness and togetherness. You must be able to talk to your sex partner before, during, and after making love. You want the object of your affection to be socially acceptable and good looking.

You see your lover as a friend and companion. You are very sexual and sensual, needing someone to appreciate and desire you. When this cannot be achieved, you have the ability to go for long periods without sexual activity. You are an expert at controlling your desires and doing without.

-D-

Once you get it into your head that you want someone, you move full steam ahead in pursuit. You do not give up your quest easily. You are nurturing and caring. If someone has a problem, this turns you on. You are highly sexual, passionate, loyal, and intense in your involvement, sometimes possessive and jealous. Sex to you is a pleasure to be enjoyed. You are stimulated by the eccentric and unusual, having a free and open mind.

-E-

Your greatest need is to talk. If your date is not a good listener, you have trouble relating. A person must be intellectually stimulating or you are not interested sexually. You need a friend for a lover and a companion for a bedmate. You hate disharmony and disruption, but you do enjoy a good argument once in a while it seems to stir things up. You flirt a lot, for the challenge is more important than the sexual act for you, but once you give your heart away, you are uncompromisingly loyal. When you don't have a good lover to fall asleep with, you will fall asleep with a good book. (Sometimes, in fact, you prefer a good book.)

-F-

You are idealistic and romantic, putting your lover on a pedestal. You look for the very best mate you can find. You are a flirt, yet once committed, you are very loyal. You are sensuous, sexual, and privately passionate. Publicly, you can be showy, extravagant, and gallant. You are born romantic. Dramatic love scenes are your favorite fantasy pastime. You can be a very generous lover.

-G-

You are fastidious, seeking perfection within yourself and your lover. You respond to a lover who is your intellectual equal or superior, and one who can enhance your status. You are sensuous and know how to reach the peak of erotic stimulation, because you work at it meticulously. You can be extremely active sexually that is, when you find the time. Your duties and responsibilities take precedence over everything else. You may have difficulty getting emotionally close to a lover, but no trouble getting close sexually.

-H-

You seek a mate who can enhance your reputation and earning ability. You will be very generous to your lover once you have attained a commitment. Your gifts are actually an investment in your partner. Before the commitment, though, you tend to be frugal in your spending and dating habits and equally cautious in your sexual involvement. You are a sensual and patient lover.

-I-

You have a great need to be loved, appreciated...Even worshipped. You enjoy luxury, sensuality, and pleasures of the flesh. You look for lovers who know what they are doing. You are not interested in an amateur, unless that amateur wants a tutor. You are fussy and exacting about having your desires satisfied. You are willing to experiment and try new modes of sexual expression. You bore easily and thus require sexual adventure and change. You are more sensual than sexual, but you are sometimes downright lustful.

-J-

You can be very romantic, attached to the glamour of love. Having a partner is of paramount importance to you. You are free in your expression of love and are willing to take chances, try new sexual experiences and partners, provided it's all in good taste. Brains turn you on. You must feel that your partner is intellectually stimulating, otherwise you will find it difficult to sustain the relationship. You require loving, cuddling, wining, and dining to know that you're being appreciated.

-K-

You are emotional and intense. When involved in a relationship, you throw your entire being into it. Nothing stops you; there are no holds barred. You are all consuming and crave someone who is equally passionate and intense. You believe in total sexual freedom when you are in love. You are willing to try anything and everything. Your supply of sexual energy is inexhaustible. You also enjoy nurturing your mate.

-L-

You are very romantic, idealistic, and somehow you believe that to love means to suffer. You wind up serving your mate or attracting people who have unusual troubles. You see yourself as your lover's savior and put your family above your own passionate needs. You are sincere, passionate, lustful, and dreamy. You can't help falling in love, and others can't help falling in love with you. You fantasize and get turned on by movies and magazines. You do not tell others of this secret life, your love for them, or of your sexual fantasies.

-M-

You are very sensitive, private, and most times sexually passive; you like a partner who takes the lead. Music, soft lights and romantic thoughts turn you on. When in love, you are romantic, idealistic, mushy, and extremely intense. You enjoy having your senses and your feelings stimulated, titillated, and teased. You are a great flirt. You tend to make your relationships fit your dreams, oftentimes all in your own head. You require constant activity, assurance and stimulation. You have tremendous physical and emotional energy and tend to always give more than your share. You are an enthusiastic lover and tend to be attractive to others. You need romance, hearts and flowers, and lots of conversation to turn you on and keep you going.

-N-

For you, it is business before pleasure. If you are in any way bothered by career, business, or money concerns, you find it very hard to relax and get into the mood. You can be romantically idealistic to a fault and are capable of much sensuality. But you never lose control of your emotions. You are very careful and cautious before you give your heart away and your body, for that matter. Once you make the commitment, though, you stick like glue.

-O-

You are very interested in sexual activities yet secretive and shy about your desires. You can re-channel much of your sexual energy into making money and/or seeking power. You can easily have extended periods of celibacy. You are a passionate, compassionate, sexual lover, requiring the same qualities from your mate. Sex is serious business; thus you demand intensity diversity, and are willing to try anything or anyone. Sometimes your passions turn to possessiveness, which must be kept in check.

-P-

You are very conscious of social proprieties. You wouldn't think of doing anything that might harm your image or reputation. Appearances count, therefore, you require a good-looking partner. You also require an intelligent partner. Oddly enough, you may view your partner as your enemy; a good fight stimulates those sex vibes. You are relatively free of sexual hang-ups. You are willing to experiment and try new ways of doing things. You are very social and sensual; you enjoy flirting and need a good deal of physical gratification.

-Q-

You are totally marvelous in bed!

-R-

You are a no-nonsense, action-oriented individual. You need someone who can keep pace with you and who is your intellectual equal the smarter the better. You are turned on more quickly by a great mind than by a great body. However, physical attractiveness is very important to you. You have to be proud of your partner. You are privately very sexy, but you do not bed, you are willing to serve as teacher. Sex is important; you can be a very demanding playmate.

-S-

You are secretive, self-contained, and shy. You are very sexy, sensual, and passionate, but you do not let on to this. Only in intimate privacy will this part of your nature reveal itself. When it gets down to the nitty-gritty, you are an expert. You know all the little tricks of the trade, can play any role or any game, and take your love life very seriously. You don't fool around. You have the patience to wait for the right person to come along.

-T-

You are enthusiastic and idealistic when in love. When not in love, you are in love with love, always looking for someone to adore. You see romance as a challenge. You are a roamer and need adventure, excitement, and freedom. You deal in potential relationships. You enjoy giving gifts and enjoy seeing your mate looking good. Your sex drive is strong and you desire instant gratification. You are willing to put your partner's pleasures above your own.

-U-

You fantasize, but do not tend to fall in and out of love easily. It is not easy for your partner to keep up with you, sexually or otherwise.

-V-

You are individualistic, and you need freedom, space, and excitement. You wait until you know someone well before committing yourself. Knowing someone means psyching him out. You feel a need to get into his head to see what makes him tick. You are attracted to eccentric, but loving types. Often there is an age difference between you and your lover. You respond to danger, thrills, and suspense. You like living on the edge sometimes. Your lover is all important to you, and you'll never let him out of your heart, for that one person means the world to you. The gay scene turns you off completely, although you don't condemn others for their desires.

-W-

You are very proud, determined, and you refuse to take no for an answer when pursuing love. Your ego is at stake. You are romantic, idealistic, and often in love with love itself, not seeing your partner as he or she really is. You feel deeply and throw all of yourself into your relationships. Nothing is too good for your lover. You enjoy playing love games.

-X-

You need constant stimulation because you bore quickly. You can handle more than one relationship at a time with ease. You can't shut off your mind. You talk while you make love. You can have the greatest love affairs, all by yourself, in your own head.

-Y-

You are sexual, sensual, and very independent. If you can't have it your way, you will forgo the whole thing. You want to control your relationships, which doesn't always work out too well. You respond to physical stimulation, enjoy necking and spending hours just touching, feeling and exploring. However, if you can spend your time making money, you will give up the pleasures of the flesh for the moment. You need to prove to yourself and your partner what a great lover you are. You want feedback on your performance. You are an open, stimulating, romantic bedmate.

-Z-

You are crap in bed.

WHAT ADULTS HAVE LEARNED.EDU

GREAT TRUTHS ABOUT LIFE THAT ADULTS HAVE LEARNED

1. Raising teenagers is like nailing JELLO to a tree.
2. There is always a lot to be thankful for if you take time to look for it. For example, I am sitting here thinking how nice it is that wrinkles don't hurt.
3. One reason to smile is that every seven minutes of every day, someone in an aerobics class pulls a hamstring.
4. The best way to keep kids at home is to make the home a pleasant atmosphere and let the air out of their tires.
5. Car sickness is the feeling you get when the monthly car payment is due.
6. Families are like fudge ... mostly sweet with a few nuts.
7. Laughing helps. It's like jogging on the inside.
8. My mind not only wanders, sometimes it leaves completely.
9. If you can remain calm, you just don't have all the facts.
10. You know you're getting old when you stoop to tie your shoes and wonder what else you can do while you're down there.

FREE STUFF.COM

(I don't know how many of these are still available, but it never hurts to try.)

PET STUFF

1.-800-331-5144 Free Triumph dog food sample

2. 1-800-524-2939 Free catbox freshener

3. 1-800-874-3221 Free petgaurd dog food sample

4. 1-800-592-6687 Free Royal canine dog food sample

5. 1-800-207-0606 Free Pro plan dog or cat food sample

6.1-800-843-4020 Free sample of "improve" canine supplement(4=coats)

7. 1-800-787-0078 Free sample of Purina tuna.

US STUFF

1. 1-800-523-9971 Free Olbas herbal cold medicine sample

2. 1-800-992-1672 Free sample of Valerian muscle relaxant

3. 1-800-547-2300 Free sample of K-Y jelly

4. 1-800-867-7258 Free sample of sea salts

5. 1-800-284-9123 Free sample of everclean shampoo

6. 1-800-383-0251 Free Ink solve hand cleaner sample

7. 1-800-297-4888 Free sample of alpha hydrox skin care

8. 1-800-645-4337 Free sample of Glide mint flavored dental floss

9. 1-888-478-7355 Free sample of purell hand sanitizer (parents=magazine)

10. 1-800-405-0800 Free lifestyles condoms

11. 1-800-733-7546 Free Vaseline sample pack

12. 1-800-354-0387 Free Gillette Sensor Excell razor

13. 1-800-746-8888 Free Zilactin medicated lip balm

14. 1-800-721-1331 Free coupon for Ciba vision contact lenses

15. 1-800-361-8068 Free sample of O.B. Tampons

16. 1-800-232-0670 Free sample of Supra C for contacts lens

17 1-800-548-3663 Free sample of Rembrante tooth paste

18. 1-800-688-3933 Free sample of Be Sure gas relief
19. 1-800-487-6526 Free sample of Ultra Pleasure condoms
20. 1-800-756-9882 Free sample of Neutrogena hand cream
21. 1-360-692-1909 Free sample of herbal phen-fen
22. 1-888-311-0020 Free depilatory cream from Cutex
23. 1-800-262-8765 Free sample of Kavatrol(supposed to relax you)
24. 1-888-767-6453 Free sample of Smile-Maxx teeth whitening tablets
25. 1-888-858-7266 Free sample of Lactaid
26. 1-888-456-7474 Free sample of Poise Bladder control pads
some more !
27. 1-800-olay-skin Free sample of Olay body wash and free puff
28. 1-800-411-5656 Free sample of UP/DOWN time herbal supplement
29. 1-888-8in-sync Free sample of IN Sync miniforms for light days
30. 1-800-226-6227 Free sample of Camo facial therapy products
31. 1-800-342-2273 Free samples of face care products from DHC
32. 1-800-448-3022 Free samples of Playtex Slim Fit tampons
33. 1-800-793-1695 Free Believers Bonus pack from Alcon(for=contacts)
34. 1-800-848-5900 Free Astro Glide personal lubricant
35. 1-800-865-8438 Free sample of Playtex Gentle Glide tampons
36. 1-800-574-2309 Free sample of Excedrin Migraine pain relief
37. 1-800-669-3275 Free sample of either lemon balm #359, organic=20
    feverfew #808, frontier clary sage #729, marshmallow root=herbs
    #610=20 (mention their web page)
38. 1-888-chr-isti Free sample of Christie Brinkley's Believe=perfume
39. 1-800-4-pepcid Free sample of Pepcid AC
40. 1-800-508-5252 Free sample of Focus contact lenses(for antistigmatism)

FOOD AND MISC. STUFF
1. 1-800-669-3275 Free sample of peppermint leaves
2. 1-888-554-3767 Free Bounty chip clip
3. 1-800-310-5662 Free sample of Colombian coffee
4. 1-800-460-7532 Free Amazon Rainforest Tea.
5. 1-800-597-2267 Free food pyramid magnet

6. 1-800-585-1300 Free book (100 action principals of the shaolin) Karate
7. 1-888-gpo-upon Free recipe book from Grey Poupon
8. 1-800-997-7358 Free sample of Vita spelt pasta.
9. 1-800-373-7226 Free sample of SACO powdered buttermilk blend?
10. 1-888-816-5491 Free sample of Enviro-Action multi purpose cleaner
11. 1-800-646-0012 Free sample 5 min phone card from Imodium AD
WE NEVER GOT A TWELVE
13. 1-800-699-4753 Free sample of tea from Water and Leaves
14. 1-800-382-8728 Free sample of Chinese slim tea.
15. 1-800-684-3322 Free calendar about Nature (members only!)
16. 1-800-964-3826 Free sample of diet tea or coffee
17. 1-888-590-6284 Free video "Women's Workout" from Reebok
18. 1-888-644-6226 Free info pack about alternative medicines
19. 1-800-833-8737 Free sample of "Happy Camper" Herbal stimulant
20. 1-800-761-9809 Free recipe board from Spice of Life

AND MORE !
Free Secret Deodorant 1-800-732-7383
Free After Bite Insect Wipes 1-888-258-4696
Free Gillette Sensor Excel Razor 1-800-354-0387
Free sample of "Believe" perfume 1-888-247-4784
Free sample Poise Pad with Side Shields 1-888-456-7474
Free 2oz Tube of Neutrogena Norwegian Formula Hand Cream 1-800-756-9882
Free sample of Excedrin Migraine Tablets and Relief Guide 1-800-301-0024
Free Bottle Baby Magic Lotion with "New Born" Coupon Package 1-800-228-7408
Free CamoCare Facial Therapy Products Sample 1-800-226-6227
Free Pregnancy Test 1-800-CARE-002
Free Dove Beauty Bar 1-800-454-7669
Free Tylenol Product Sample 1-800-962-5357

Free Promotional Sports Cards 1-800-220-8179
Free sample of Cinnamon Theraflu 1-888-368-2624
Free Opti-Free-free Contac Lens Protein Remover 1-800-354-4972
Plank Road Music Sampler 1-800-437-0832
Free Dental Floss 1-800-645-4337
Free TransUnion Credit Report (Recently Denied Credit Applicants Only) 1-800-916-8800
Free Color Soft Shampoo 1-888-390-6866
Free "Squirrel Away" Powder Sample 1-800-229-5454
Free Towelette tooth wipe sample 1-888-WE-SMILE
Free Snapple Drink 1-800-SNAPPLE
Free Nescafe Coffee 1-800-637-2233
Free Herbal Tea 1-800-373-3832
Free Style Beans 1-800-200-9272
Free Crayola Stain Removal Guide 1-800-272-9652
Free Post-It Notes for Ink-Jet & Laser Printers 1-800-330-3966
Free Magnetic Bounty Snack Bag 1-888-554-3767
Free Information on ANY US Government Agency, Service or Program 1-800-688-9889
Free Adobe Image Library Browser Demo CD-ROM 1-888-502-8393
Free Aveeno Skin Lotion 1-888-428-3366
Free Edge Pro Gel Sample 1-888-368-1305
Free Purina One Dog Food 1-800-787-0078 x40
Free Peach Ice Tea Crystal Light 1-800-562-3434
Free Pepcid Sample 1-800-473-7243
Free Beano 1-800-257-8650
Free Trial Issue of "House Beautiful" Magazine (cancel after 1)1-800-285-7060
Free Trial Issue of "Chili Peppers" Cooking Magazine (cancel after 1) 1-800-767-9377
Free sample of "Journey Perfume"-A new fragrance from Mary Kay 1-800-788-1238 (1)

Free sample of Purell Hand Sanitizer 1-888-478-7355
and more !
Free Lifestyles Condom sample and Info Booklet 1-800-405-0080
Free sample of "TPR"—Therapeutic Pain Rub 1-800-959-1007
Free Oil of Olay Moisturizing Body Wash sample and Free Puff Ball
(0.7oz) 1-800-652-9754
Free sample "N-ZYME5"–A Natural Digestive Enzyme Product 1-
800-247-773
Free 4-Day Trial of HT-400 Weight Loss Supplement 1-800-447-8841=
Free sample of "Recourse" Nutritional Drink- Chocolate or Vanilla 1-
800-952-3880
Free Gordon's Seafood Recipes Booklet 1-800-222-6846
Free sample of "Vita-Spelt" Grain Baking Product 1-800-997-7358
Free 700 Club "Fact Sheet" from The Christian Broadcast Network 1-
800-716-3228
Free 1998 EDF "Wonders of Wildlife" Calendar 1-800-684-3322
Free Pledge Coupon 1-888-647-5334
Free Max Factor Lasting Performance Foundation 1-800-810-0875
Free Advanced Curad Aqua-Protect Bandage sample and $1.00 Coupon
1-888-682-4587
THE LIST- Free Advertising! Tell them Annette had you call for even
more offers 1-800-781-9644
Free (3oz) sample of Rembrandt Toothpaste! 1-800-548-3663
Free sample of Dad's Brand Premium Puppy Food 1-800-600-3237
Free Ziploc Baggie's Money Saving Coupons 1-800-428-4795
Goodnights from Huggies 1-800-583-9966
NutraSweet E-Z Survival Kit 1-800-632-8935
SoftLens 66 Contact Lenses 1-800-583-7778
Free Similac Baby Formula Sample 1-800-222-9546
Disney Vacation Planning Video 1-800-453-4844
Cutex Ultra Nail Lacquer 1-800-335-2243
Trial Pack of O.B. Applicator Tampons 1-800-361-8068

Sweet Success Meal Planner 1-800-318-8730

Free Coupon and Recipes from The McCormick Spice Company 1-800-632-5847

Free "Miracle Whip Cooks" Recipes Booklet from Kraft 1-800-523-4660

Free 3-pc sampler of Old-Tyme Sugar-Free Taffy 1-800-874-0261

Breathe-Right Nasal Strips sample and $1.50 Coupon 1-800-858-6673

Free "Celebrity Skin Care Secrets" Booklet from Vaseline 1-888-449-8477

Free sample of Nutra Cell Nutritional Supplements/Vitamins 1-888-592-9229

Free Saco Powdered Buttermilk Blend Mix 1-800-373-7226

Free Neutraceutical Slim Diet Coffee or Tea Sample 1-800-964-3826

Free Slimfits Tampons from Playtex 1-800-448-3022

Free Oral B Nickelodeon Rugrats Toothpaste Sample 1-800-577-5952

if that's not enough, here's more !

Free InSyne Miniform Feminine Protection Product 1-888-846-7962

Louisiana Tourism Vacation Kit 1-800-41-GUMBO

Free Good Seasonings Roasted Garlic Salad Dressing Sample 1-800-874-6586

Free Kimlan Soy Sauce 1-800-FREE-SOY

Free Mai tonic tea sample 1-800-747-7418

Free Sample EverClean Shampoo 1-800-284-9123

Free Sample Computer Labels 1-888-283-7972 x144 (this one works!)

Free Victoria's Secret Catalog 1-800-HER-GIFT

Free Curel Lotion 1-800-287-3597

Cycletrol Cat Litter Box Freshener 1-800-542-2939

Free Odorless Garlic(kyalic) 1-800-688-3933

Free Ocushist Eye Drops 1-888-628-4478

Free Ensure Sample 1-800-986-8535

Free Gerber "Dices" Sample 1-800-443-7237

Free Halogen Light Bulb Cover 1-800-985-2220

Free Cortexx Shampoo Sample 1-888-CORTEXX

Ink Solv30 hand cleaner Sample 1-800-383-0251

Free Resolve Carpet Cleaner Brush 1-800-781-8778

Free Naturally Soft Sample 1-888-311-0020

Free CD-ROM Trial Edition of "Quick Books" Accounting Software from Quicken 1-888-226-7300

Free Lever 2000 Anti-bacterial Soap 1-800-418-2453

Free Food Pyramid Magnet 1-800-597-2267

Free Redbook "Women's Training" Workout CD-ROM 1-888-590-6284

Free Loft's Grass Seeds 1-888-775-6387

Free Poster of Sherrie Austin, Country Singer 1-888-374-3774

Free Martin Luther King, Jr. "Living The Dream" Poster 1-800-729-6686

Free "Nestles Quik Sticker" from Nestles 1-888-758-7766

Free $1.50 Coupon off Purchase of Colgate Platinum Toothpaste 1-800-962-2345

Free "Cooking with Cranberries" Recipe Booklet from Ocean Spray 1-800-662-3263

Free "Inventor's Kit"—Everything You need To Patent Your Invention 1-800-977-7100

Free Swanson Low-Fat "Make-Over" Recipes Booklet 1-800-479-2676

Free A-1 Original Steak Sauce "Discover The Flavors" Free Recipe Booklet 1-800-217-3247

Free Wisk Pretreater Sample 1-800-ASK-WISK

Need to Settle a Dispute call TV'S JUDGE JUDY 1-888-800-JUDY

Free "Tyvek" Mailing Envelopes Sampler Pack from DuPont 1-800-448-9835

Free Outlet Mall Helpline-Brochures, Maps and Info on Nationwide Outlet Malls 1-800-336-8853

Free 10-Minute Phone Card from Canadian Whiskey 1-888-890-8028

Free 5-Minute Phone Card from Imodium Advanced (for short survey) 1-800-646-0012

can there be this many ?

Free sample of "Nixalite"-Protect Your Property from Pest Birds 1-800-624-1189

Free Waterbed Conditioner and Catalog 1-800-495-7533

Free Ferry-Morse Flower Seed Pack and Newsletter—Join the Free "Garden Club" 1-800-283-3400

Free sample of "SepticCare" for Septic Tank/Cesspool Systems 1-800-621-6065

Home Energy Saving Kit 1-800-GET-PINK

Free '98 Pet Calendar 1-800-294-1400 (press 1) try for a 2000 calendar.

Free Video on GERD Disease & Heartburn 1-800-HT-BURN

State Farms "Working Woman's Wedding Planner" 1-888-733-8368

Free Booklet "All Vitamins Are Not Equal" 1-800-937-0500 (x1690)

Free Breast Exam Shower Card 1-888-227-5552

ABC Network Free Drug Guide for Children 1-800-222-3329

Free Sample of Zilactin Baby Teething Medicine 1-800-746-8888

Free Catalog-Great Christian Books 1-800-775-5422

Free Video from Century21 Remodeling 1-800-685-8554

Free Eden Pasta Recipe Brochure 1-800-248-0302

Free Vitamin Guide 1-800-992-8451 (xNAH1)

Free Recipes & Coupons from EdenSoy 1-888-424-EDEN

Hormel Recipes & Coupon Booklet 1-800-523-4635

Collection of Bread Machine Recipes 1-800-373-7226

Free Land'O'Lakes Cheese Recipes 1-800-782-9602

Oscar Meyer Bologna Recipes 1-800-522-9477 (x0012)

Sargento's Cheese Recipes 1-800-223-7702

Cream of Wheat Free Recipes 1-888-HOT-CEREAL

Camel Cigarette Premiums 1-800-226-3522

Virginia Slims Catalog 1-800-868-9327

Basic Cigarette Premiums Catalog 1-800-343-0975

Merit Cigarette Premiums Catalog 1-800-884-5777

Carlton Cigarette Premiums Catalog 1-800-569-3781

Spice For Life 18 page recipe book 1-800-761-9809

Free Sample Cervital Antioxidant 1-800-831-9505

M&M's Recipe Booklet 1-800-627-7852

Campbells Soup Recipes 1-800-401-SOUP
Sports One Supplement Samples 1-800-624-8787
USA Rice Council Recipes 1-800-795-7423
King Arthur Flour Recipes Catalog 1-800-777-4434
Free Ranch Style Beans 1-800-382-6363
Mrs.Dash Recipe Club 1-800-622-3274
ho hum !
Ro-Tel Recipe Booklet 1-800-544-5680
Free Sample of Godet White Chocolate 1-888-879-4633
Near East Rice Recipe Booklet 1-800-399-4488
Free Sample of NutraSalt 1-800-206-9454
Alaska Salmon Recipes & Offers 1-800-LUV-SAMN
Brochure Car Care Tips 1-800-9-FIRESTONEFree Subscription to
the "Ultress Insider" 1-888-4-ULTRESS
Vitasona Product Coupon 1-888-VITAL-US
Myrtle Beach Vacation Planner 1-800-356-3016
Free NordicTrac Video 1-800-441-2371
Just My Size Catalog & Coupons 1-800-978-FITS
Take A Bite Out Of Crime Comic Book 1-800-627-2911
Sample of Curtail anti-gas med.for your pet 1-800-257-8650
Grey Poupon Classic Recipes 1-800-GP-DIJON
Free activity book from MooTown Snackers 1-800-243-3737
Free sample EZ-QUI Household Cleaner 1-800-847-4526
Kraft 2% cheese recipe booklet 1-800-659-0683
Mazola Corn Oil recipe brochures 1-800-338-8831
Merrick Dog Food Snacks 1-800-936-3354
Free Closet Design Video 1-800-200-9272
Join Triaminic Parent's Club 1-888-935-5543
Free Video "Taking Charge of Your TV"" 1-800-452-6351
Free sample of Phisoderm Face Wash 1-888-TRY-PHISO
Free 1998 Calendar from Sun Up Gallery 1-888-887-8687
Pepperidge Farm Pastry Recipes 1-800-762-8301

Del Monte Tomato Recipe Booklet 1-800-244-5616
Free Lactaid Ultra Sample 1-888-858-7266
Carnation quick fix recipes 1-800-240-9424
Living With Asthma Booklet 1-800-722-4337
Free Video on Nail Fungus 1-800-928-7374
Take Control of Diabetes Video 1-800-517-4411
Free Weight Loss Cassette 1-800-511-3357
Equal Cooking Recipes and Coupons 1-800-323-5316
Foster & Smith Puppy Training Guide 1-800-826-7206
Join Doral & Co. For Coupons & Offers 1-800- 743-6725
Free Microflex Surgical Latex Gloves 1-800-876-6866
Free Sega CD-ROM 1-888-734-2736
Hearing Loss Video & Booklet 1-800-896-6400
Gerber Baby Food Coupons 1-800-443-7237
Free Cruise Planner 1-888-Y-CRUISE
Join K-Mart's Baby of Mine Club 1-800-533-0143
Free Riunite Wine Guide 1-888-407-4864
Chinese Herbals $15 worth of Coupons 1-800-877-1704
Business Success Kit 1-800-255-6380
Teach Your Dog To Play Frisbee 1-888-444-ALPO
Free Ezo Denture Adhesive 1-800-476-2252
Free Printer Paper Samples from Avery 1-888-283-7972 (Ext.144)
Free Child Safety Kit (Polly Klaas Foundation) 1-800-587-HELP
Get your FREE sample of ThermoLift (This product is for losing weight) 1-888-225-9872 (Ext.1535)
Free sample of Fanas Pain Relief Cream 1-800-957-5513
Free Information Kit for Cookbook Fund Raising 1-800-227-728
Free Charleston,SC Beach Guide 1-800-868-8118

BABY STUFF
1. 1-800-222-9546 Free starter pack of Similac formula.
2. 1-800-505-2742 Free SIDS video, sticker, and babysitter reminder
3. 1-800-577-5952 Free sample of oral-b Rugrats toothpaste

4. 1-800-443-7237 Free sample of Gerber baby dices
5. 1-800-969-5268 Free sample of Children's chewable Mylanta.
6. 1-800-care-002 Free pregnancy test=20
wow, I guess that's the end ! whew, that was a trip !
IF YOU SAVED A BUNDLE LET ME KNOW

TREES, TREES, TREES.EDU

See which tree your birthday falls under, then look at descriptions at bottom of this message. Interesting

December 23 to January 1	Apple Tree
January 2 to January 11	Fir Tree
January 12 to January 24	Elm Tree
January 25 to February 3	Cypress Tree
February 4 to February 8	Poplar Tree
February 9 to February 18	Cedar Tree
February 19 to February 28	Pine Tree
March 1 to March 10	Weeping Willow Tree
March 11 to March 20	Lime Tree
March 21	Oak Tree
March 22 to March 31	Hazelnut Tree
April 1 to April 10	Rowan Tree
April 11 to April 20	Maple Tree
April 21 to April 30	Walnut Tree
May 1 to May 14	Poplar Tree
May 15 to May 24	Chestnut Tree
May 25 to June 3	Ash Tree
June 4 to June 13	Hornbeam Tree
June 14 to June 23	Fig Tree
June 24	Birch Tree
June 25 to July 4	Apple Tree
July 5 to July 14	Fir Tree

July 15 to July 25	Elm Tree
July 26 to August 4	Cypress Tree
August 5 to August 13	Poplar Tree
August 14 to August 23	Cedar Tree
August 24 to September 2	Pine Tree
September 3 to September 12	Weeping Willow Tree
September 13 to September 22	Lime Tree
September 23	Olive Tree
September 24 to October 3	Hazelnut Tree
October 4 to October 13	Rowan Tree
October 14 to October 23	Maple Tree
October 24 to November 11	Walnut Tree
November 12 to November 21	Chestnut Tree
November 22 to December 1	Ash Tree
December 2 to December 11	Hornbeam Tree
December 12 to December 21	Fig Tree
December 22	Beech Tree

APPLE Tree, the Love

Of slight build, lots of charm, appeal and attraction, pleasant aura, flirtatious, adventurous, sensitive, always in love, wants to love and be loved, faithful and tender partner, very generous, scientific talents, lives for today, a carefree philosopher with imagination.

FIR Tree, the Mysterious

Extraordinary taste, dignity, cultivated airs, loves anything beautiful, moody, stubborn, tends to egoism but cares for those close to it, rather modest, very ambitious, talented, industrious uncontent lover, many friends, many foes, very reliable.

ELM Tree, the Noble-Mindedness

Pleasant shape, tasteful clothes, modest demands, tends to not forgive mistakes, cheerful, likes to lead but not to obey, honest and faithful partner, tends to a know-all-attitude and making decisions for others, noble-minded, generous, good sense of humor, practical.

CYPRESS, the Faithfulness

Strong, muscular, adaptable, takes what life has to give, happy content, optimistic, needs enough money and acknowledgment, hates loneliness, passionate lover which cannot be satisfied, faithful, quick-tempered, unruly, pedantic and careless.

POPLAR, the Uncertainty

Looks very decorative, no self-confident behavior, only courageous if necessary, needs goodwill and pleasant surroundings, very choosy, often lonely, great animosity, artistic nature, good organizer, tends to philosophy, reliable in any situation, takes partnership serious.

CEDAR, the Confidence

Of rare beauty, knows how to adapt, likes luxury, of good health not in the least shy, tends to look down on others, self-confident, determined, impatient, wants to impress others, many talents, industrious, healthy optimism, waiting for the one true love, able to make quick decisions.

PINE Tree, the Particularity

Loves agreeable company, very robust, knows how to make life comfortable, very active, natural, good companion, but seldom friendly, falls easily in love but its passion burns out quickly, gives up easily, many disappointments till it finds its ideal, trustworthy, practical.

WEEPING WILLOW, the Melancholy

Beautiful but full of melancholy, attractive, very empathic, loves anything beautiful and tasteful, loves to travel, dreamer, restless, capricious, honest, can be influenced but is not easy to live with, demanding, good intuition, suffers in love but finds sometimes an anchoring partner.

LIME Tree, the Doubt

Accepts what life dishes out in a composed way, hates fighting, stress and labor, tends to laziness and idleness, soft and relenting, makes sacrifices for friends, many talents but not tenacious enough to make them blossom, often wailing and complaining, very jealous, loyal.

HAZELNUT Tree, the Extraordinary

Charming, undemanding, very understanding, knows how to make an impression, active fighter for social cause, popular, moody and capricious lover, honest and tolerant partner, precise sense of judgment.

ROWAN, the Sensitivity

Full of charm, cheerful, gifted, without egoism, likes to draw attention, loves life, motion, unrest and even complications, is both dependent and independent, good taste, artistic, passionate, emotional, good company, does not forgive.

MAPLE, Independence of Mind

No ordinary person, full imagination and originality, shy and reserved, ambitious, proud, self-respect, hungers for new experiences, sometimes nervous, many complexes, good memory, learns easily, complicated love life, wants to impress.

WALNUT Tree, the Passion

Unrelenting, strange and full of contrasts, often egoistic, aggressive, noble, broad horizon, unexpected reactions, spontaneous, unlimited ambition, no flexibility, difficult and uncommon partner, not always liked but often admired, ingenious strategist, very jealous and passionate, no compromises.

CHESTNUT Tree, the Honesty

Of unusual beauty, does not want to impress, well-developed sense of justice, vivacious, interested, a born diplomat, but irritate and sensitive in company, often due to a lack of self-confidence, acts sometimes superior, feels not understood loves only once, has difficulties in finding a partner.

ASH Tree, the Ambition

Uncommonly attractive, vivacious, impulsive, demanding, does not care for criticism, ambitious, intelligent, talented, likes to play with its fate, can be egoistic, very reliable and trust- worthy, faithful and prudent lover, sometimes brains rule over heart, but takes partnership very serious.

HORNBEAM, the good taste

Of cool beauty, cares for its looks and condition, good taste, tends to egoism, makes life as comfortable as possible, leads reasonable, disciplined life, looks for kindness, an emotional partner and acknowledgment, dreams of unusual lovers, is seldom happy with her feelings, mistrusts most people, is never sure of its decisions, very conscientious.

FIG Tree, the Sensibility

Very strong, a bit self-willed, independent, does not allow contradiction or arguments, loves life, its family, children and animals, a bit of a butterfly, good sense of humor, likes idleness and laziness, of practical talent and intelligence.

OAK, robust nature

Courageous, strong, unrelenting, independent, sensible, does not love changes, keeps its feet on the ground, person of action.

BIRCH, the Inspiration

Vivacious, attractive, elegant, friendly, unpretentious, modest, does not like anything in excess, abhors the vulgar, loves life in nature and in calm, not very passionate, full of imagination, little ambition, creates a calm and content atmosphere.

OLIVE Tree, the Wisdom

Loves sun, warmth and kind feelings, reasonable, balanced, avoids aggression and violence, tolerant, cheerful, calm, well-developed sense of justice, sensitive, empathic, free of jealousy, loves to read and the company of sophisticated people.

BEECH, the Creative

Has good taste, concerned about its looks, materialist, good organization of life and career, economical, good leader, takes no unnecessary risks, reasonable, splendid lifetime companion, keen on keeping fit (diets, sports, etc.).

OUT OF THE MOUTHS OF BABES.EDU

One summer evening during a violent thunderstorm a mother was tucking her small boy into bed. She was about to turn off the light when he asked with a tremor in his voice, "Mommy, will you sleep with me tonight?" The mother smiled and gave him a reassuring hug. "I can't, dear," she said. "I have to sleep in Daddy's room." A long silence was broken at last by his shaky little voice: "The big sissy."

~ ~ ~ ~ ~

A mother took her three-year-old daughter to church for the first time. the church lights were lowered, and then the choir came down the aisle, carrying lighted candles. All was quiet until the little one started to sing in a loud voice, "Happy birthday to you, Happy birthday to you...."

~ ~ ~ ~ ~

Nine-year-old Joey was asked by his mother what he had learned in Sunday School. "Well, Mom, our teacher told us how God sent Moses behind enemy lines on a rescue mission to lead the Israelites out of Egypt. When he got to the Red Sea, he had his engineers build a pontoon bridge, and all the people walked across safely. He used his walkie-talkie to radio headquarters and call in an airstrike. They sent in bombers to blow up the bridge and all the Israelites were saved." "Now, Joey, is that REALLY what your teacher taught you?" his mother asked "Well, no, Mom, but if I told it the way the teacher did, you'd never believe it!"

~ ~ ~ ~ ~

A child came home from Sunday School and told his mother that he had learned a new song about a cross-eyed bear named Gladly. It took his mother a while before she realized that the hymn was really "Gladly The Cross I'd Bear."

~ ~ ~ ~ ~

It was that time during the Sunday morning service for "the children's sermon," and all the children were invited to come forward. One little girl was wearing a particularly pretty dress and, as she sat down, pastor leaned over and said to her, "That is a very pretty dress. it your Easter dress?" The little girl replied, directly into the pastor's clip-on microphone, "Yes, and my Mom says it's a Bitch to iron."

~ ~ ~ ~ ~

Finding one of her students making faces at others on the playground, Ms. Smith stopped to gently reprove the child. Smiling sweetly, teacher said, "Bobby, when I was a child, I was told that if I made faces, it would freeze and It would stay like that." Bobby looked up and replied, "Well, Ms Smith, you can't say you weren't warned."

~ ~ ~ ~ ~

My friend likes to read his two young sons fairy tales at night. Having a deep-rooted sense of humor, he often ad-libs parts of the stories for fun. One day his youngest son was sitting in his first grade class while the teacher was reading the story of the Three Little Pigs. She came to the part of the story where the first pig was trying to acquire building materials for his home. She said, "And so the pig went up to the man with a wheelbarrow full of straw and said, "Pardon me sir, but might I have some of that straw with which to build my house?"

Then the teacher asked the class, "And what do you think the man said?"My friend's son raised his hand and said, "I know! I know! He said "Holy smokes! A talking pig!"

The teacher was unable to teach for the next 10 minutes.

~ ~ ~ ~ ~

A Sunday school teacher was discussing the Ten Commandments with her five and six year olds. After explaining the commandment to "honor thy Father and thy mother," she asked, "Is there a commandment that teaches us how to treat our brothers and sisters?" Without missing a beat one little boy (the Oldest of a family) answered, "Thou shall not kill."

~ ~ ~ ~ ~

An honest seven-year-old admitted calmly to her parents that Billy Brown had kissed her after class. "How did that happen?," gasped her mother. "It wasn't easy," admitted the young lady, "but three girls helped me catch him."

~ ~ ~ ~ ~

One day a little girl was sitting and watching her mother do the dishes at the kitchen sink. She suddenly noticed that her mother has several strands of white hair sticking out in contrast on her brunette head. She looked at her mother and inquisitively asked, "Why are some of your hairs white, Mom?" Her mother replied, "Well, every time that you do something wrong and make me cry or unhappy, one of my hairs turns white." The little girl thought about this revelation for a while and then said, "Momma, how come ALL of grandma's hairs are white?"

~ ~ ~ ~ ~

A three-year-old went with his dad to see a litter of kittens. On returning home, he breathlessly informed his mother that there were two boy kittens and two girl kittens. "How did you know?" his mother asked. "Daddy picked them up and looked underneath," he replied, "I think it's printed on the bottom."

~ ~ ~ ~ ~

The children had all been photographed, and the teacher was trying to persuade them each to buy a copy of the group picture. "Just think how nice it will be to look at it when you are all grown up and say, 'There's Jennifer; she's a lawyer,' or 'That's Michael. He's a doctor.'" A small voice at the back of the room rang out, "And there's the teacher. She's dead."

A teacher was giving a lesson on the circulation of the blood. Trying to make the matter clearer, he said, "Now, boys, if I stood on my head, the blood, as you know, would run into it, and I would turn red in the face." "Yes, sir," the boys said. "Then why is it that while I am standing upright in the ordinary position, the blood doesn't run into my feet?" A little fellow shouted, "'Cause yer feet ain't empty."

For weeks, a six-year old lad kept telling his first-grade teacher about the baby brother or sister that was expected at his house. One day the mother allowed the boy to feel the movements of the unborn child. The six-year old was obviously impressed, but he made no comment. Furthermore, he stopped telling his teacher about the impending event. The teacher finally sat the boy on her lap and said, "Tommy, whatever has become of that baby brother or sister you were expecting at home?" Tommy burst into tears and confessed, "I think Mommy ate it!"

On the first day of school, the Kindergarten teacher said, "If anyone has to go to the bathroom, hold up two fingers." A little voice from the back of the room asked, "How will that help?

A kindergarten teacher was observing her classroom of children while they drew. She would occasionally walk around to see each child's artwork.

As she got to one little girl who was working diligently, she asked what the drawing was.

The girl replied, "I'm drawing God."

The teacher paused and said, "but no one knows what God looks like." Without missing a beat, or looking up from her drawing the girl replied, "They will in a minute."

～　～　～　～　～

Last week I took my children to a restaurant. My six-year-old son asked if he could say grace. As we bowed our heads, he said, "God is good. God is great. Thank you for the food, and I would even thank you more if Mom gets us ice cream for dessert. And liberty and justice for all! Amen!".

Along with laughter from the other customers nearby, I heard a woman remark, "That's what's wrong with this country. Kids today don't even know how to pray. Asking God for ice cream! Why, I never!".

Hearing this, my son burst into tears and asked me, "Did I do it wrong? Is God mad at me?". As I held him and assured him that he had done a terrific job and God was certainly not mad at him, an elderly gentleman approached the table. He winked at my son and said, "I happen to know that God thought that was a great prayer.". "Really?", my son asked. "Cross my heart.", he said. Then in a theatrical whisper the gentleman added (indicating the woman whose remark had started this whole thing), "Too bad she never asks God for ice cream. A little ice cream is good for the soul sometimes.".

Naturally, I bought my kids ice cream at the end of the meal. My son stared at his for a moment and then did something I will remember the rest of my life. He picked up his sundae and without a word walked over and placed it in front of the woman. With a big smile he told her, "Here, this is for you. Ice cream is good for the soul sometimes, and my soul is already good.".

BEGIN THE YEAR WITH A GRIN... Out of the mouths of babes.org

1. A Sunday school teacher asked her little children, as they were on the way to church service, "And why is it necessary to be quiet in church?" One bright little girl replied, "Because people are sleeping."

2. A little boy opened the big and old family Bible with fascination, looking at the old pages as he turned them. Then something fell out of the Bible and he picked it up and looked at it closely. It was an old leaf from a tree that has been pressed in between the pages. "Momma, look what I found," the boy called out. "What have you got there, dear?" his mother asked. With astonishment in the young boy's voice he answered, "It's Adam's suit!!"

3. The preacher was wired for sound with a lapel mike, and as he preached, he moved briskly about the platform, jerking the mike cord as he went. Then he moved to one side, getting wound up in the cord and nearly tripping before jerking it again. After several circles and jerks, a little girl in the third pew leaned toward her mother and whispered, "If he gets loose, will he hurt us?"

4. My grandson was visiting one day when he asked, "Grandma, do you know how you and God are alike?" I mentally polished my halo while I asked, "No, how are we alike?" "You're both old," he replied.

5. A ten-year old, under the tutelage of her grandmother, was becoming quite knowledgeable about the Bible. Then one day she floored her grandmother by asking, "Which Virgin was the mother of Jesus? The virgin Mary or the King James Virgin?"

6. A Sunday school class was studying the Ten Commandments. They were ready to discuss the last one. The teacher asked if anyone could tell her what it was. Susie raised her hand, stood tall, and quoted, "Thu shall not take the covers off the neighbor's wife."

7. I had been teaching my three-year old daughter, Caitlin, the Lord's Prayer. For several evenings at bedtime, she would repeat after me the lines from the prayer. Finally, she decided to go solo. I listened

with pride as she carefully enunciated each word, right up to the end of the prayer: "Lead us not into temptation," she prayed, "but deliver us some E-mail. Amen."

8. A little boy was in a relative's wedding. As he was coming down the aisle, he would take two steps, stop, and turn to the crowd. While facing the crowd, he would put his hands up like claws and roar. So it went, step, step, ROAR, step, step, ROAR, all the way down the aisle. As you can imagine, the crowd was near tears from laughing so hard by the time he reached the pulpit. The little boy, however, was getting more and more distressed from all the laughing, and was also near tears by the time he reached the pulpit. When asked what he was doing, the child sniffed and said, "I was being the Ring Bear."

9. One Sunday in a Midwest city, a young child was "acting up" during the morning worship hour. The parents did their best to maintain some sense of order in the pew but were losing the battle. Finally, the father picked the little fellow up and walked sternly up the aisle on his way out. Just before reaching the safety of the foyer, the little one called loudly to the congregation, "Pray for me! Pray for me!"

10. And one particular four-year old prayed, "And forgive us our trash baskets as we forgive those who put trash in our baskets."

11. One student's prayer: "Now I lay me down to rest, And hope to pass tomorrow's test. If I should die before I wake, That's one less test I have to take."

12. A little boy was overheard praying: "Lord, if you can't make me a better boy, don't worry about it. I'm having a real good time like I am."

Out of the Mouth of Other Babes.com

TEACHER: Tommy, why do you always get so dirty?
 TOMMY: Well, I'm a lot closer to the ground then you are.

TEACHER: Why are you late?
WEBSTER: Because of the sign.
TEACHER: What sign?
WEBSTER: The one that says, "School Ahead, Go Slow."

SILVIA: Dad, can you write in the dark?
FATHER: I think so. What do you want me to write?
SYLVIA: Your name on this report card.

TEACHER: In this box, I have a 10-foot snake.
SAMMY: You can't fool me, Teacher...snakes don't have feet.

TEACHER: How can you prevent diseases caused by biting insects?
JOSE: Don't bite any.

TEACHER: Ellen, give me a sentence starting with "I".
ELLEN: I is...
TEACHER: No, Ellen. Always say, "I am."
ELLEN: All right..."I am the ninth letter of the alphabet."

MOTHER: Why on earth did you swallow the money I gave you?
JUNIOR: You said it was my lunch money.

TEACHER: If I had seven oranges in one hand and eight oranges in the other, what would I have?
CLASS COMEDIAN: Big hands

ON THE LIGHT SIDE.COM

Sherlock Holmes and Dr. Watson went on a camping trip. After a good meal and a bottle of wine they lay down for the night, and went to sleep. Some hours later, Holmes awoke and nudged his faithful friend. "Watson, look up at the sky and tell me what you see." Watson replied, "I see millions and millions of stars." "What does that tell you?" Watson pondered for a minute. "Astronomically, it tells me that there are millions of galaxies and potentially billions of planets. Astrologically, I observe that Saturn is in Leo. Chronologically, I deduce that the time is approximately a quarter past three. Theologically, I can see that God is all powerful and that we are small and insignificant. Meteorologically, I suspect that we will have a beautiful day tomorrow. What does it tell you?" Holmes was silent for a minute, then spoke. "Watson, you imbecile. Someone has stolen our tent."

Do not walk behind me, for I may not lead. Do not walk ahead of me, for I may not follow. Do not walk beside me, either. Just leave me the hell alone.

The journey of a thousand miles begins with a broken fan belt and a leaky tire.

It's always darkest before dawn. So if you're going to steal the neighbor's newspaper, that's the time to do it.

It's a small world. So you gotta use your elbows a lot.

Sex is like air: it's not important unless you aren't getting any.

It is far more impressive when others discover your good qualities without your help.

If you think nobody cares if you're alive, try missing a couple of car payments.

If you tell the truth you don't have to remember anything. If you lend someone $20, and never see that person again, then it probably was worth it.

If you haven't much education you must use your brain.

You can't strengthen the weak by weakening the strong.

Who gossips to you will gossip of you.

When someone says, "Do you want my opinion?"—it's always a negative one.

When someone is having a bad day, be silent, sit close by and nuzzle them gently.

The word listen contains the same letters as the word silent.

The trouble with work is—it's so daily.

The difference between ordinary and extraordinary is that little extra.

Scientists say one out of every four people is crazy. Check three friends and if they are OK, then you're it.

Pain and suffering is inevitable but misery is optional.

On The Deeper Side.com

The Paradox of our Time—George Carlin

The paradox of our time in history is that we have taller buildings, but shorter tempers; wider freeways, but narrower viewpoints.

We spend more, but have less; we buy more, but enjoy it less. We have bigger houses and smaller families; more conveniences, but less time; we have more degrees, but less sense; more knowledge, but less judgment; more experts, but more problems; more medicine, but less wellness.

We drink too much, smoke too much, spend too recklessly, laugh too little, drive too fast, get too angry too quickly, stay up too late, get up too tired, read too seldom, watch TV too much, and pray too seldom.

We have multiplied our possessions, but reduced our values. We talk too much, love too seldom, and hate too often. We've learned how to make a living, but not a life; we've added years to life, not life to years. We've been all the way to the moon and back, but have trouble crossing the street to meet the new neighbor.

We've conquered outer space, but not inner space. We've done larger things, but not better things.

We've cleaned up the air, but polluted the soul.

We've split the atom, but not our prejudice.

We write more, but learn less.

We plan more, but accomplish less.

We've learned to rush, but not to wait.

We build more computers to hold more information to produce more copies than ever, but have less communication.

These are the times of fast foods and slow digestion; tall men, and short character; steep profits, and shallow relationships.

These are the times of world peace, but domestic warfare, more leisure, but less fun; more kinds of food, but less nutrition.

These are days of two incomes, but more divorce; of fancier houses, but broken homes.

These are days of quick trips, disposable diapers, throw-away morality, one-night stands, overweight bodies, and pills that do everything from cheer to quiet, to kill. It is a time when there is much in the show window and nothing in the stockroom; a time when technology can bring this letter to you, and a time when you can choose either to share this insight, or to just hit delete.

George Carlin

"A citizen of America will cross the ocean to fight for democracy, but won't cross the street to vote in a national election."—Bill Vaughan

We yell for the Government to balance the budget, then take the last dime we have to make the down payment on a car that will take 5 years to pay off.

We demand speed laws that will stop fast driving, then won't buy a car if it can't go over 100 miles an hour.

We know the line-up of every baseball team in the American and National Leagues but mumble through half the words in the "Star Spangled Banner".

We'll spend half a day looking for vitamin pills to make us live longer, then drive 90 miles an hour on slick pavement to make up for lost time.

We tie up our dog while letting our sixteen year old son run wild.

We whip an enemy in battle, then give them the shirt off our backs.

We will work hard on a farm so we can move into town where we can make more money so we can move back to the farm.

We get upset we're spending over a billion dollars for education, but spend three billion dollars a year for cigarettes.

In the office we talk about baseball, shopping or fishing, but when we are out at the game, the mall or on the lake, we talk about business.

We're supposed to be the most civilized Christian nation on earth, but we still can't deliver payrolls without an armored car.

We have more experts on marriage than any other country in the world and still have more divorces.

We're the country that has more food to eat than any other country in the world and more diets to keep us from eating it.

and

We have taller buildings, but shorter tempers;
wider freeways, but narrower viewpoints;
we spend more, but have less;
we buy more, but enjoy it less.

We have bigger houses and smaller families;
more conveniences, but less time;
we have more degrees, but less common sense;
more knowledge, but less judgement;
more experts, but more problems;
more medicine, but less wellness.

We spend too recklessly,
laugh too little, drive too fast,
get too angry too quickly,
stay up too late, get up too tired,
read too seldom, watch TV too much,

and pray too seldom.

We have multiplied our possessions,

We've conquered outer space, but not inner space;
we've done larger things, but not better things;
we've cleaned up the air, but polluted the soul;

we've split the atom, but not our prejudice;
we write more, but learn less;
plan more, but accomplish less.

We've learned to rush, but not to wait;
we have higher incomes; but lower morals;
more food but less appeasement;
more acquaintances, but fewer friends;
more effort but less success.

We build more computers to hold more information,
to produce more copies than ever,
but have less communication;
we've become long on quantity,
but short on quality.

These are the time of fast foods and slow digestion;
tall men and short character;
steep profits, and shallow relationships.

These are the times of world peace, but domestic warfare;
more leisure and less fun;
more kinds of food, but less nutrition.

These are days of two incomes, but more divorce;
of fancier houses, but broken homes.

Author Unknown

As you got up this morning.org
I watched you,
and hoped you would talk to me,

even if it was just a few words,
asking my opinion or thanking me
for something good that happened
in your life yesterday.

But I noticed you were too busy,
trying to find the right outfit to wear.
When you ran around the house getting ready,
I knew there would be a few minutes
for you to stop and say hello,
but you were to busy.

At one point you had to wait,
fifteen minutes with nothing to do
except sit in a chair.
Then I saw you spring to your feet.
I thought you wanted to talk to me
but you ran to the phone and called a friend
to get the latest gossip instead.
I watched patiently all day long.
With all your activities
I guess you were too busy to say
anything to me.

I noticed that before lunch you looked around,
maybe you felt embarrassed to talk to me,
that is why you didn't bow your head.
You glanced three or four tables over
and you noticed some of your friends
talking to me briefly before they ate, but you didn't.
That's okay.

There is still more time left,
and I hope that you will talk to me yet.
You went home and it seems as if
you had lots of things to do.
After a few of them were done,
you turned on the TV.

I don't know if you like TV or not,
just about anything goes there
and you spend a lot of time
each day in front of it
not thinking about anything,
just enjoying the show.
I waited patiently again
as you watched the TV and ate your meal,
but again you didn't talk to me.
Bedtime I guess you felt too tired.
After you said goodnight to your family
you plopped into bed and fell asleep in no time.
That's okay because you may not realize
that I am always there for you.

I've got patience,
more than you will ever know.
I even want to teach you how
to be patient with others as well.
I love you so much that I wait
everyday for a nod, prayer or thought
or a thankful part of your heart.

It is hard to have a one-sided conversation.
Well, you are getting up once again.

And once again I will wait,
with nothing but love for you.

Hoping that today you will give me some time.
Have a nice day!
Your friend,
GOD

MEMO.ORG

To: YOU
Date: TODAY
From: THE BOSS
Subject: YOURSELF
Reference: LIFE

I am God. Today I will be handling all of your problems. Please remember that. I do not need your help. If life happens to deliver a situation to you that you cannot handle, do not attempt to resolve it. Kindly put it in the SFGTD (something for God to do) box. It will be addressed in My time, not yours. Once the matter is placed into the box, do not hold on to it.

If you find yourself stuck in traffic; Don't despair. There are people in this world for whom driving is an unheard of privilege.

Should you have a bad day at work; Think of the man who has been out of work for years.

Should you despair over a relationship gone bad; Think of the person who has never known what it's like to love and be loved in return.

Should you grieve the passing of another weekend; Think of the woman in dire straits, working twelve hours a day, seven days a week to feed her children.

Should your car break down, leaving you miles away from assistance; Think of the paraplegic who would love the opportunity to take that walk.

Should you notice a new gray hair in the mirror; Think of the cancer patient in chemo who wishes she had hair to examine.

Should you find yourself at a loss and pondering what is life all about, asking what is my purpose? Be thankful. There are those who didn't live long enough to get the opportunity.

Should you find yourself the victim of other people's bitterness, ignorance, smallness or insecurities; Remember, things could be worse. You could be them!!!!

CLASS OF 2003.ORG

1. Most of this years students were born in 1981.
2. They are the first generation born into Luvs, Huggies, and Pampers.
3. John Lennon and John Belushi have always been dead.
4. There has always been a woman on the supreme Court, and women have always been traveling into space.
5. They have never needed a prescription to buy ibuprofen.
6. They never realized that for one brief moment, Gen. Alexander Haig was " in charge."
7. They never heard Walter Cronkite suggest that "that's the way it is."
8. They were born and grew up with Microsoft, IBM PCs, in-line skates, Nutrasweet, fax machines, film on disks, and unregulated quantities of commercial interruptions on television.
9. Somebody named Dole has always been running for something.
10. Cats has been on Broadway all their lives.
11. Although they all know her children, they have no idea who "ma Bell' was.
12. They never heard anyone say, "Book em, Dan-O, Good night John-boy" or "kiss my grits," in prime time.
13. They never knew Madonna when she was like a virgin.
14. Mike Myers is the 'Spy Who Shagged Me', not the first congressman expelled from the body in a century for his role in "abscam."
15. They never had to worry about the packaging of Tylenol.
16. Yugoslavia has never existed.
17. They have never seen Bob Marley perform reggae live.
18. Jessie Jackson has always been getting someone out of trouble someplace.
19. Strikes by highly paid athletes have been a routine part of professional athletics.

20. The moonwalk is a Michael Jackson dance step, not a Neil Armstrong giant step.
21. Travel to space has always been accomplished in reusable spacecraft.
22. John Cougar has always been John Cougar Mellencamp, or vice versa.
23. The term "adult" has increasing come to mean "dirty."
24. The year they were born, reports condemned violence on television and in Hollywood films for producing the likes of John Hinckley.
25. They have always been able to get their news from USA Today and CNN.
26. They have spent more than half their lives with Bart Simpson.
27. They don't understand why Solidarity is spelled with a capital "S".
28. They don't think there is anything terribly futuristic about 2001, and were never concerned about the year 1984.
29. They have no idea how big a breadbox is.
30. Camelot refers to King Arthur's seat of government, not President Kennedy's.
31. Kennedy's assassination is as significant to them as that of Lincoln or Garfield.
32. They have probably never dialed a phone or opened as icebox.
33. The only thing a 'churchkey' has ever opened for the is a church.
34. They have never seen white smoke over the Vatican and do not know its significance.
35. They cannot identify the last United States president to throw-up on a Japanese prime minister.
36. Ketchup has always been a vegetable.
37. Susan B. Anthony has always been on the dollar but probably never bought them anything.
38. They cannot imagine waiting a generation to get the dirt on the U.S. president.
39. They felt pretty special when their elementary school had top-of-the-line Commodore 64s.

40. ET, Gremlins, and The Hulk provided their Halloween costumes and lunch-box themes.
41. They were introduced to Kramer on the TV show 'Friday's.'
42. They remember when 'Saturday Night Live' was still funny.
43. They have never seen a Bank-Americard.

PRISON VS. WORK.com

In prison you spend the majority of your time in an 8' X 10' cell.
At work you spend most of your time in a 6' X 8' cubicle.

In prison you get three meals a day.
At work you only get a break for one meal and you have to pay for that one.

In prison you get time off for good behavior.
At work you get rewarded for good behavior with more work.

In prison a guard locks and unlocks all the doors for you.
At work you must carry around a security card and unlock and open all the doors yourself.

In prison you can watch TV and play games.
At work you get fired for watching TV and playing games.

In prison they ball-and-chain you when you go somewhere.
At work you are just ball-and-chained.

In prison they allow your family and friends to visit.
At work you cannot even speak to your family and friends.

In prison all expenses are paid by taxpayers, with no work required.
At work you get to pay all the expenses to go to work and then they deduct taxes from your salary to pay for the prisoners.

In prison you spend most of your life looking through bars from the inside wanting to get out.

At work you spend most of your time wanting to get out and inside bars.

In prison you can join many programs which you can leave at any time.
At work there are some programs you can never get out of.

In prison there are wardens who are often sadistic.
At work we have managers.

NOTICE TO ALL EMPLOYEES EFFECTIVE JANUARY 1, Y2K.com

Effective January 1, Y2K, the following guidelines are to be followed regarding employees missing work.

SICKNESS

We will no longer accept your doctor's statements as proof. We believe if you are able to go to the doctor, you are able to work.

LEAVE OF ABSENCE FOR SURGERY

We are no longer allowing this practice. As long as you are employed here, you will need all of whatever you have and should not consider having anything removed. We hired you as you are, and to have anything removed would certainly make you less than we bargained for. Anyone having operations will be FIRED immediately.

PREGNANCY

In the event of extreme pregnancy, you will be allowed to go to the first aid room when the pains are FIVE MINUTES apart. If it is false labor, you will have to take an hour's leave without pay.

DEATH

This will be accepted as an excuse, BUT we would like 2 weeks notice, as we feel it is your duty to teach someone your job.

From,

THE MANAGEMENT

HoW To KeEp A HeaLthY LeVel Of iNsAniTy aNd dRiVe OtHeR PeOple iNsAnE.cOm

1) At lunch time, sit in your parked car and point a hair dryer at passing cars to see if they slow down

2) Page yourself over the intercom. (Don't disguise your voice.)

3) Insist that your e-mail address be xena-goddess-of-fire@companyname.com

4) Every time someone asks you to do something, ask if they want fries with that.

5) Encourage your colleagues to join you in a little synchronized chair dancing.

6) Put your garbage can on your desk and label it 'IN'.

7) Develop an unnatural fear of staplers.

8) Put decaf in the coffee maker for 3 weeks. Once everyone has gotten over their caffeine addictions, switch to espresso.

9) In the memo field of all your checks, write 'for sexual favors.'

10) Reply to everything someone says with, "That's what you think."

11) Finish all your sentences with "In accordance with the prophecy".

12) Adjust the tint on your monitor so that the brightness level lights up the entire work area. Insist to others that you like it that way.

13) dontuseanypunctuationorspaces

14) As often as possible, skip rather than walk.

15) Ask people what sex they are.

16) Specify that your drive-through order is "to go".

17) Sing Along at the opera.

18) Go to a poetry recital and ask why the poems don't rhyme.

19) Find out where your boss shops and buy exactly the same outfits. Wear them one day after your boss does. (This is especially effective if your boss is the opposite gender.)

20) Send e-mail to the rest of the company to tell them where you're going. For example: If anyone needs me, I'll be in the bathroom.

21) Put mosquito netting around your cubicle

22) Five days in advance, tell your friends you can't attend their party because you're not in the mood.

23) Hum when you ride an elevator.

JOB APPLICATION

This is from an actual job application a 17 year old boy submitted at a McDonald's fast-food establishment in Florida and they hired him because he was so honest and funny!

NAME: Craig Bilmush

Sex: Not yet. Still waiting for the right person.

DESIRED POSITION: Company's President or Vice President. But seriously, whatever's available. If I was in a position to be picky, I wouldn't be applying here in the first place.

DESIRED SALARY: $185,000 a year plus stock options and a Michael Ovitz style severance package. If that's not possible, make an offer and we can haggle.

EDUCATION: Yes.

LAST POSITION HELD: Target for middle management hostility.

SALARY: Less than I'm worth.

MOST NOTABLE ACHIEVEMENT: My incredible collection of stolen pens and post-it notes

REASON FOR LEAVING: It sucked.

HOURS AVAILABLE TO WORK: Any.

PREFERRED HOURS: 1:30-3:30 p.m., Monday, Tuesday, and Thursday.

DO YOU HAVE ANY SPECIAL SKILLS?: Yes, but they're better suited to a more intimate environment.

MAY WE CONTACT YOUR CURRENT EMPLOYER?: If I had one, would I be here?

DO YOU HAVE ANY PHYSICAL CONDITIONS THAT WOULD PROHIBIT YOU FROM LIFTING UP TO 50 LBS?: Of what?

DO YOU HAVE A CAR?: I think the more appropriate Question here would be "Do you have a car that runs?".

HAVE YOU RECEIVED ANY SPECIAL AWARDS OR RECOGNITION?: I may already be a winner of the Publishers Clearing house Sweepstakes.

DO YOU SMOKE?: On the job no, on my breaks yes.

WHAT WOULD YOU LIKE TO BE DOING IN FIVE YEARS?: Living in the Bahamas with a fabulously wealthy dumb sexy blonde super model who thinks I'm the greatest thing since sliced bread. Actually, I'd like to be doing that now.

DO YOU CERTIFY THAT THE ABOVE IS TRUE AND COMPLETE TO THE BEST OF YOUR KNOWLEDGE?: Yes. Absolutely. SIGN HERE: Aries

Rules for Work

1. Never give me work in the morning. Always wait until 4:00 and then bring it to me. The challenge of a deadline is refreshing.
2. If it's really a rush job, run in and interrupt me every 10 minutes to inquire how it's going. That helps. Or even better, hover behind me, advising me at every keystroke.
3. Always leave without telling anyone where you're going. It gives me a chance to be creative when someone asks where you are.
4. If my arms are full of papers, boxes, books, or supplies, don't open the door for me. I need to learn how to function as a paraplegic and opening doors with no arms is good training in case I should ever be injured and lose all use of my limbs.
5. If you give me more than one job to do, don't tell me which is priority. I am psychic.
6. Do your best to keep me late. I adore this office and really have nowhere to go or anything to do. I have no life beyond work.
7. If a job I do pleases you, keep it a secret. If that gets out, it could mean a promotion.

8. If you don't like my work, tell everyone. I like my name to be popular in conversations. I was born to be whipped.

9. If you have special instructions for a job, don't write them down. In fact, save them until the job is almost done. No use confusing me with useful information.

10. Never introduce me to the people you're with. I have no right to know anything. In the corporate food chain, I am plankton. When you refer to them later, my shrewd deductions will identify them.

11. Be nice to me only when the job I'm doing for you could really change your life and send you straight to manager's hell.

12. Tell me all your little problems. No one else has any and it's nice to know someone is less fortunate. I especially like the story about having to pay so much taxes on the bonus check you received for being such a good manager.

13. Wait until my yearly review and THEN tell me what my goals SHOULD have been. Give me a mediocre performance rating with a cost of living increase. I'm not here for the money anyway.

More work stuff

Be sure to read through to the bottom…

1 Bob Smith, my assistant programmer, can always be found
2 hard at work in his cubicle. Bob works independently, without
3 wasting company time talking to colleagues. Bob never
4 thinks twice about assisting fellow employees, and he always
5 finishes given assignments on time. Often he takes extended
6 measures to complete his work, sometimes skipping coffee
7 breaks. Bob is a dedicated individual who has absolutely no
8 vanity in spite of his high accomplishments and profound
9 knowledge in his field. I firmly believe that Bob can be
10 classed as a high-caliber employee, the type which cannot be
11 dispensed with. Consequently, I duly recommend that Bob be
12 promoted to executive management, and a proposal will be

13 executed as soon as possible.

Addendum:

That idiot was standing over my shoulder while I wrote the report sent to you earlier today. Kindly re-read only the odd numbered lines.

PONDERANCES.COM

Subject: Thoughts for pondering and for having a chuckle or two.com

Remember, amateurs built the ark. Professionals built the Titanic.

Conscience is what hurts when everything else feels so good.

Talk is cheap because supply exceeds demand.

Stupidity got us into this mess—why can't it get us out?

Love is grand; divorce is a hundred grand.

Even if you are on the right track, you'll get run over if you just sit there.

Politicians and diapers have one thing in common. They should both be changed regularly and for the same reason.

An optimist thinks that this is the best possible world. A pessimist fears that this is true.

There is always death and taxes; however death doesn't get worse every year.

People will accept your ideas much more readily if you tell them that Benjamin Franklin said it first.

It's easier to fight for one's principles than to live up to them.

I don't mind going nowhere as long as it's an interesting path.

Anything free is worth what you pay for it.

Indecision is the key to flexibility.

It hurts to be on the cutting edge.

If it ain't broke, fix it till it is.

I don't get even, I get odder.

In just two days, tomorrow will be yesterday.

I always wanted to be a procrastinator, never got around to it.

Dijon vu—the same mustard as before.

I am a nutritional overachiever.

My inferiority complex is not as good as yours.

I am having an out of money experience.

I plan on living forever. So far, so good.

I am in shape. Round is a shape.

Not afraid of heights—afraid of widths.

Practice safe eating—always use condiments.

A day without sunshine is like night.

I have kleptomania, but when it gets bad I take something for it.

If marriage were outlawed, only outlaws would have in-laws.

I am not a perfectionist. My parents were though.

Life is an endless struggle full of frustrations and challenges, but eventually you find a hair stylist you like.

You're getting old when you get the same sensation from a rocking chair that you once got from a roller coaster.

One of life's mysteries is how a two pound box of candy can make a woman gain five pounds.

It's frustrating when you know all the answers, but nobody bothers to ask you the questions.

The real art of conversation is not only to say the right thing at the right time, but also to leave unsaid the wrong thing at the tempting moment.

Time may be a great healer, but it's also a lousy beautician.

Brain cells come and brain cells go, but fat cells live forever.

Age doesn't always bring wisdom, Sometimes age comes alone.

Life not only begins at forty, it begins to show.

You don't stop laughing because you grow old, you grow old because you stopped laughing.

CHRISTMAS STORIES.COM

Is there a Santa Clause?.com

(Highly Scientific Thesis)

1) No known species of reindeer can fly. However there are 300,000 species of living organisms yet to be classified, and while most of these are insects and germs, this does not completely rule out flying reindeer which only Santa has ever seen.

2) There are 2 billion children (persons under 18) in the world. However, since Santa doesn't appear to handle most Muslim, Hindu, and Buddhist children, that reduces the workload to 15% of the total—378 million according to Population Reference Bureau. At an average rate of 3.5 children per household (according to the census bureau), that makes 91.8 million homes. We'll presume that there is at least one "good" child in each.

3) Santa has 31 hours of Christmas to work with thanks to the different time zones and the rotation of the earth, assuming he travels east to west which seems logical). This works out to 822.6 visits per second. In other words, for each Christian household with "good" children Santa has 1/1000th of a second to: park, hop out of the sleigh, jump down the chimney, fill the stockings, distribute the remaining presents under the tree, eat whatever snacks have been left, get back up the chimney, get back into the sleigh, and move on to next house. Assuming that each of these 91.8 million stops are evenly distributed around the earth (which, of course is false but for the purpose of our calculations we will accept), we are now talking about .78 miles per household, a total trip of 75.5 million miles, not counting stops to

do what most of us must do at least once every 31 hours. This means that Santa's sleigh is moving at 650 miles per second, or 3000 times the speed of sound. For purposes of comparison, the fastest man made vehicle ever invented, the Ulysses space probe, moves at a poky 27.4 miles per second. A conventional reindeer can only run 15 miles per hour, tops.

4) The payload on the sleigh adds another interesting element. Assuming that each child gets nothing more than a medium-sized Lego set (2 pounds), the sleigh is carrying 321,300 tons, not counting Santa, who is already overweight and stuffed by the end of the night with milk and cookies from 91.8 million homes. On land a conventional team of reindeer can pull no more than 300 pounds. Even granting that "flying reindeer" can pull ten times that amount, Santa needs 214,200 reindeer to do the job. This increases the payload—not even counting the weight of the sleigh itself—to 354,430 tons. Again, for purposes of comparison, this is four times the weight of the cruise ship Queen Elizabeth II.

5) 353,000 tons traveling at 650 miles per second creates enormous air resistance, which will heat the reindeer up in the same fashion as a spacecraft reentering the earth's atmosphere. The lead pair of reindeer will each absorb 14.3 quintillion (14,300,000,000,000,000,000) joules of energy per second, instantaneously bursting into flames, creating deafening sonic booms in their wake, and exposing the reindeer following them to the same forces. The entire reindeer team will be vaporized within 4.26 thousandths of a second. Meanwhile, Santa will be subjected to acceleration forces over 17,500 times greater than gravity. A 250 pound Santa will be pinned to the back of his sleigh by 4,315,015 pounds of force. The only sound conclusion from the above is, if Santa ever did deliver presents on Christmas Eve, he's now certainly dead. Those Aussies sure know how to tell a Barbie and Ken joke. To wit, these letters to Santa, are from a children's author in Melbourne:

Barbie's Letter To Santa.com

Dear Santa,

Listen you fat troll, I've been saving your ass every year, being the perfect Christmas Present, wearing skimpy bathing suits in December and dressing in fake Chanel at sappy tea parties. I hate to break it to ya', Santa, but it's payback time. There had better be some changes around here, or I'm gonna call for a nationwide meltdown, and trust me, you don't wanna be around to smell it. These are my demands for Christmas 1999:

1. Sweat pants and an oversized sweatshirt. I'm sick of looking like a hooker in hot pink bikinis. Do you have any idea what it feels like to have nylon and velcro up your butt? I don't suppose you do.
2. Real underwear that can be pulled on and off. That cheap-o molded underwear some genius at Mattel came up with looks like cellulite!
3. A REAL man…I don't care if you have to go to Hasbro to get him, bring me GI JOE. Hell, I'd take Tickle-Me-Elmo over that pathetic bump of a boytoy, Ken. And what was up with that earring anyway? HULLO!?!
4. It's about time you made us all anatomically correct. Give me arms that actually bend so I can push the aforementioned Ken-wimp away once he is anatomically correct.
5. Breast reduction surgery. 'Nuff said.
6. A jog-bra. To wear until I get the surgery.
7. A new career. Pet doctor and school teacher make real money.
8. A new, more 90s persona. Maybe "PMS Barbie," complete with a pint of cookie dough ice cream and a bag of chips.
9. No more McDonald's endorsements. The grease is wrecking my vinyl complexion.
10. Mattel stock options. It's been 40 years—I think I deserve a piece of the action.

Considering my valuable contribution to society and Mattel, I think these demands are reasonable. If you don't like it, you can find yourself a new bitch for next Christmas.

It's that simple.
As ever, Barbie

Ken's Letter To Santa.com

Dear Santa.

It has come to my attention that one of my colleagues has petitioned you for changes in her contract, specifically asking for anatomical and career changes. In addition, it is my understanding that disparaging remarks were made about me, my sexuality, and some of my fashion choices.

I would like to take this opportunity to inform you of issues concerning Ms. Barbie, as well as some of my own needs and desires: First, I, along with several of my colleagues, feel Ms. Barbie DOES NOT deserve the preferential treatment she has received over the years. That bitch has everything!! Neither I, nor Joe, Jem or The Raggedys, Ann & Andy, have dreamhouses, Corvettes, dune buggies, evening gowns; some of us don't even have the ability to change our hairstyle!! I have had a limited wardrobe-obviously designed to complement but never upstage Ms. Barbie! My decision to accessorize with an earring was immediately quashed, which I protest, for it was my decision and reflects my lifestyle choice!

I would like a change in my career to further explore my creative nature. Some options which could be considered are, "Decorator Ken,", "Beauty Salon Ken," or "Broadway Ken." Other avenues which could be considered are: "Go-Go Ken," "Impersonator Ken" (with wigs and gowns), or "West Hollywood Ken." These would more accurately reflect my interests and, I believe, open up markets that have been underserved.

As for Ms. Barbie needing bendable arms so she can "push me away", I need bendable knees so I can kick the bitch to the curb. In closing, further concessions to the Blonde Bimbo from Hell, while the needs of others within my coalition are ignored, will result in legal action to be taken by myself and others.

Sincerely, Ken

Christmas Carols for the Psychologically Challenged.org

SCHIZOPHRENIA:

Do you Hear What I Hear?

MULTIPLE PERSONALITY DISORDER:

We Three Queens Disoriented Are

DEMENTIA:

I Think I'll Be Home for Christmas

NARCISSISTIC:

Hark the Herald Angels Sing About Me

MANIC:

Deck the Halls and Walls and House and Lawn and Streets and Stores and Office and Town and Cars and Busses and Trucks and Trees and Fire Hydrants and…

PARANOID:

Santa Claus is Coming to Get Me.

PERSONALITY DISORDER:

You Better Watch Out, I'm Gonna Cry, I'm Gonna Pout, Maybe I'll tell you Why.

DEPRESSION:

Silent Anhedonia, Holy Anhedonia, All is Flat, All is Lonely.

OBSESSIVE-COMPULSIVE DISORDER:

Jingle Bell, Jingle Bell, Jingle Bell Rock, Jingle Bell, Jingle Bell, Jingle Bell Rock, Jingle Bell, Jingle Bell, Jingle Bell Rock, Jingle Bell, Jingle Bell, Jingle Bell Rock, Jingle Bell, Jingle Bell, Jingle Bell Rock, Jingle Bell, Jingle Bell, Jingle Bell Rock.(better start again)

PASSIVE-AGGRESSIVE PERSONALITY:

On the First Day of Christmas My True Love Gave to Me (and then took it all away).

BORDERLINE PERSONALITY DISORDER:

Thoughts of Roasting on an Open Fire

WHAT ME WORRY?.COM

Two Things Not to Worry About.com

In my life, I have found there are two things about which I should never worry. First, I shouldn't worry about the things I can't change. If I can't change them, worry is certainly most foolish and useless. Second, I shouldn't worry about the things I can change. If I can change them, then taking action will accomplish far more than wasting my energies in worry. Besides, it is my belief that, 9 times out of 10, worrying about something does more danger than the thing itself. Give worry its rightful place—out of your life.

This diet is designed to help you cope with the stress that builds up during the holiday season.

> Breakfast:
>> 1 grapefruit
>> 1 slice whole wheat toast
>> 8 oz. skim milk
>
> Lunch:
>> 4 oz. lean broiled chicken breast
>> 1 cup steamed spinach
>> 1 cup herb tea.
>> 1 Oreo cookie
>
> Mid-Afternoon snack:
>> The rest of Oreos in the package
>> 2 pints Rocky Road ice cream, nuts, cherries and whipped cream
>> 1 jar hot fudge sauce
>
> Dinner:
>> 2 loaves garlic bread

4 cans or 1 large pitcher Coke

1 large sausage, mushroom and cheese pizza.

3 Snickers bars

Late Evening News:

Entire frozen Sara Lee cheesecake (eaten directly from freezer)

Rules for this Diet

1. If you eat something and no one sees you eat it, it has no calories.
2. If you drink a diet soda with a candy bar, the calories in the candy bar are canceled out by the diet soda.
3. When you eat with someone else, calories don't count if you do not eat more than they do.
4. Food used for medicinal purposes NEVER count, such as hot chocolate, brandy, toast and Sara Lee Cheesecake.
5. If you fatten up everyone else around you, then you look thinner.
6. Movie related foods do not have additional calories because they are part of the entertainment package and not part of one's personal fuel. (Examples: Milk Duds, buttered popcorn, Junior Mints, Red Hots, and Tootsie Rolls.)
7. Cookie pieces contain no calories. The process of breaking causes calorie leakage.
8. Things licked off knives and spoons have no calories if you are in the process of preparing something.
9. Foods that have the same color have the same number of calories and is the lesser of the two. (Examples are: spinach and pistachio ice cream; mushrooms and mashed potatoes.)
10. Chocolate is a universal color and may be substituted for any other food color.
11. Anything consumed while standing has no calories. This is due to gravity and the density of the caloric mass.

12.Anything consumed from someone else's plate has no calories since the calories rightfully belong to the other person and will cling to his/her plate. (We ALL know how calories like to cling!)

REMEMBER: STRESSED SPELLED BACKWARDS IS DESSERTS!

Just Fun Things To Do.com

Things to do in an Elevator.com

1) When there's only one other person in the elevator, tap them on the shoulder and then pretend it wasn't you.

2) Push the buttons and pretend they give you a shock. Smile, and go back for more.

3) Ask if you can push the button for other people, but push the wrong ones.

4) Call the Psychic Hotline from your cell phone and ask if they know what floor you're on.

5) Hold the doors open and say you're waiting for your friend. Then let the doors close and say, "Hi Greg. How's it goin'?"

6) Drop a pen and wait until someone reaches to help pick it up, then scream, "That's mine!"

7) Bring a camera and take pictures of everyone in the elevator.

8) Move your desk in to the elevator and whenever someone gets on, ask if they have an appointment.

9) Lay down a Twister mat and ask people if they'd like to play.

10) Leave a box in the corner, and when someone gets on ask them if they hear something ticking.

11) Pretend you are a flight attendant and review emergency procedures and exits with the passengers.

12) Ask, "Did you feel that?"

13) Stand really close to someone, sniffing them occasionally.

14) When the doors close, announce to the others, "It's okay. Don't panic, they open up again."

15) Swat at flies that don't exist.

16) Tell people that you can see their aura.

17) Call out, "group hug!", then enforce it.

18) Grimace painfully while smacking your forehead and muttering "Shut up, all of you, just shut up!"

19) Crack open your briefcase or purse, and while peering inside, ask, "Got enough air in there?"

20) Stand silently and motionless in the corner, facing the wall, without getting off.

21) Stare at another passenger for a while, then announce in horror, "You're one of THEM" and back away slowly.

22) Wear a puppet on your hand and use it to talk to the other passengers.

23) Listen to the elevator walls with a stethoscope.

24) Make explosion noises when anyone presses a button.

25) Stare, grinning at another passenger for a while, and then announce, "I have new socks on."

26) Draw a little square on the floor with chalk and announce to the other passengers, "This is my personal space".

Ways to have an Extra-Specially Fun Time in a department store.com

Get boxes of condoms and randomly put them in people's carts when they don't realize it.

Set all the alarm clocks to go off at ten minute intervals throughout the day.

Try on bras on top of your clothes.

Walk up to an employee and tell him/her in an official tone "I think we've got a code 3 in housewares," and see what happens.

Tune all the radios to obnoxious stations; then turn them all off and turn the volumes to 10.

Re-dress the mannequins as you see fit.

Test the fishing rods and see what you can "catch" from the other aisles.

Move "Caution: wet floor" signs to the carpet.

Nonchalantly "test" the brushes and combs in cosmetics.

Look right into the security camera and use it as a mirror for picking your nose.

Take up an entire aisle in toys by setting up a miniature battlefield with GI Joes vs. X-Men.

Switch the men's and women's signs on the restrooms.

Dart around suspiciously while humming the theme from "Mission Impossible."

Set up a "valet parking" sign at the front door.

In the auto department, practice your Madonna look with the funnels.

Hide in the clothing racks and when people browse through say things like "pick me pick me" and scare them into believing that the clothes are talking to them.

Go to an empty checkout line and try to check people out.

Drag a lounge chair on display over to the magazines and relax.

50 Fun Things to do in a Mall.com

1. Ride mechanical horses with coins fished out of the fountain.
2. Try pants on backwards at the Gap. Ask the salesperson if they make your butt look big.
3. Dial 900 numbers from demonstration phones in Radio Shack.
4. Sneeze on the sample tray at Hickory Farms and helpfully volunteer to consume its now unwanted contents.
5. At the bottom of an escalator, scream 'MY SHOELACES! AAAGH!'
6. Ask the sales personnel at the music store whether inflated CD prices are in pesos or rubles.
7. Teach pet store parrots new vocabulary that makes them unsellable.
8. Stomp on ketchup packets at Burger King…
9. …but save a few to slurp on as snacks. Tell people that they're 'astronaut food'.

10. Follow patrons of B. Dalton's around while reading aloud from 'Dianetics.'
11. Ask mall cops for stories of World War I.
12. Ask a salesman why a particular TV is labeled black and white and insist that it's a color set. When he disagrees, give him a strange look and say, 'You mean you really can't see it?'
13. Construct a new porch deck in the tool department of Sears.
14. Wear pancake makeup and new clothes and pose as a fashion dummy in clothes departments, occasionally screaming without warning.
15. Test mattresses in your pajamas.
16. Ask the tobacconist if his hovercraft is full of eels.
17. If you're patient, stare intently into a surveillance camera for an hour while rocking from side to side.
18. Sprint up the down escalator.
19. Stare at static on a display TV and challenge other shoppers whether they, too, can see the 'hidden picture'.
20. Ask appliance personnel if they have any TVs that play only in Spanish.
21. Make unusual requests at the Piercing Pagoda.
22. Ask a salesperson in the hardware department how well a particular saw cuts through bone.
23. At the pet store, ask if they have bulk discounts on gerbils, and whether there's much meat on them.
24. Hula dance by the demonstration air conditioner.
25. Ask for red-tinted lenses at the optometrist.
26. Sneak up on saleswomen at the perfume counter and spray *them* with your own bottle of Eau de Swane.
27. Rummage through the jelly bean bin at the candy store, insisting that you lost a contact lens.
28. Ask a saleswoman whether a particular shade of panties matches the color of your beard.
29. In the changing rooms, announce in a singsong voice, 'I see London, I see France...'

30. Leave on the plastic string connecting a new pair of shoes, and wander around the mall taking two-inch steps.
31. Play the tuba for change.
32. Ask the Hammond organ dealer if he can play 'Jesus Built My Hotrod'.
33. Record belches on electronic sampling keyboards, and perform gastric versions of Jingle Bells for admiring onlookers.
34. Ask the pharmacist at the drugstore which leading cold remedy will 'give you a really wicked buzz'.
35. Ask the personnel at Pier 1 Imports whether they have 'any giant crap made out of straw'.
36. 'Toast' plastic gag hot dogs in front of the fake fireplace display.
37. Collect stacks of paint brochures and hand them out as religious tracts.
38. Ask the information desk for a stroller, and someone to push you around in it.
39. Change every TV in the electronics department to a station showing 'Saved by the Bell'. Chant the dialogue in a robotic voice, and scream if anyone tries to switch channels on one of the sets.
40. Hang out in the waterbed section of the furniture department wearing a Navy uniform. Occasionally run around in circles yelling 'scratch one flattop!'
41. Hand a stack of pants back to the changing room attendant and scornfully announce that none of them are 'leak proof'.
42. 'Play' the demo modes of video games at the arcade. Make lots of explosion noises.
43. Stand transfixed in front of a mirror bobbing your head up and down.
44. Pay for all your purchases with two-dollar bills to provoke arguments over whether they're real.
45. If it's Christmas, ask the mall Santa to sit on *your* lap.
46. Answer any unattended service phones that ring in department stores and say 'Domino's.'
47. Try on flea collars at the pet store while occasionally pausing to scratch yourself.

48. At the stylist, ask to have the hair on your back permed.
49. Show people your driver's license and demand to know 'whether they've seen this man.'
50. Buy a jawbreaker from the candy store. Return fifteen minutes later, fish it out of your mouth, and demand to know why it hasn't turned blue yet.

Books.edu

Children's books that didn't quite make it.edu

You Are Different and That's Bad
   The Boy Who Died From Eating All His Vegetables
   Dad's New Wife Robert
   Fun four-letter Words to Know and Share
   The Kids' Guide to Hitchhiking
   Curious George and the High-Voltage Fence
   The Little Sissy Who Snitched
   Some Kittens Can Fly.
   The Magic World Inside the Abandoned Refrigerator
   The Pop-Up Book of Human Anatomy
   Strangers Have the Best Candy
   Whining, Kicking and Crying to Get Your Way
   You Were an Accident
   Things Rich Kids Have, But You Never Will
   Pop! Goes The Hamster…And Other Great Microwave Games
   The Man in the Moon Is Actually Satan
   Your Nightmares Are Real
   Eggs, Toilet Paper, and Your School
   Why Can't Mr. Fork and Ms. Electrical Outlet Be Friends?
   Places Where Mommy and Daddy Hide Neat Things
   Daddy Drinks Because You cry

THE WORLD'S SHORTEST BOOKS.edu

   20. HOW TO LAND A PLANE AT MARTHA'S VINEYARD by JFK, Jr.

19. HOW TO PLEASE WOMEN by John Bobbit
18. MY PLAN TO FIND THE REAL KILLERS by O. J. Simpson
17. THE ENGINEER'S GUIDE TO FASHION
16. TO ALL THE MEN I'VE LOVED BEFORE by Ellen DeGeneres
15. HUMAN RIGHTS ADVANCES IN CHINa.
14. THINGS I WOULD NOT DO FOR MONEY by Dennis Rodman
13. THE WILD YEARS by Al Gore
12. AMELIA EARHART'S GUIDE TO THE PACIFIC OCEAN
11. AMERICA'S MOST POPULAR LAWYERS
10. CAREER OPPORTUNITIES FOR LIBERAL ARTS MAJORS
9. DIFFERENT WAYS TO SPELL BOB
8. DR. KEVORKIAN'S COLLECTION OF MOTIVATIONAL SPEECHES
7. EVERYTHING MEN KNOW ABOUT WOMEN
6. EVERYTHING WOMEN KNOW ABOUT MEN
5. FRENCH HOSPITALITY
4. GEORGE FOREMAN'S BIG BOOK OF BABY NAMES
3. MIKE TYSON'S GUIDE TO DATING ETIQUETTE
2. THE AMISH PHONE DIRECTORY
And the Number one World's Shortest book:…
1. THE BOOK OF VIRTUES by Bill Clinton

HOUSEHOLD HINTS.COM

Some helpful hints.com

Yeah, they're on there also.

1) Stuff a miniature marshmallow in the bottom of a sugar cone to prevent ice cream drips.

2) Use a meat baster to "squeeze" your pancake batter onto the hot griddle perfectly-shaped pancakes every time.

3) To keep potatoes from budding, place an apple in the bag with the potatoes.

4) To prevent egg shells from cracking, add a pinch of salt to the water before hard-boiling

5) Run your hands under cold water before pressing Rice Krispies treats in the pan-the marshmallow won't stick to your fingers

6) To get the most juice out of fresh lemons, bring them to room temperature and roll them under your palm against the kitchen counter before squeezing.

7) To easily remove burnt-on food from your skillet, simply add a drop or two of dish soap and enough water to cover bottom of pan, and bring to a boil on stove-top-skillet will be much easier to clean.

8) Spray your Tupperware with nonstick cooking spray before pouring in tomato-based sauces—no more stains.

9) When a cake recipe calls for flouring the baking pan, use a bit of the dry cake mix instead—no white mess on the outside of the cake.

10) If you accidentally over-salt a dish while it's still cooking, drop in a peeled potato—it absorbs the excess salt for an instant "fix me up."

11) Wrap celery in aluminum foil when putting in the refrigerator it will keep for weeks.

12) Brush beaten egg white over pie crust before baking to yield a beautiful glossy finish.

13) Place a slice of apple in hardened brown sugar to soften it back up.

14) When boiling corn on the cob, add a pinch of sugar to help bring out the corn's natural sweetness.

15) To determine whether an egg is fresh, immerse it in a pan of cool, salted water. If it sinks, it is fresh—if it rises to the surface, throw it away.

16) Cure for headaches: Take a lime, cut it in half and rub it on your forehead. The throbbing will go away.

17) Don't throw out all that leftover wine: Freeze into ice cubes for future use in casseroles and sauces.

18) If you have a problem opening jars: Try using latex dishwashing gloves. They give a non-slip grip that makes opening jars easy.

19) Potatoes will take food stains off your fingers. Just slice and rub raw potato on the stains and rinse with water.

20) To get rid of itch from mosquito bite: try applying soap on the area, instant relief.

21) Ants, ants, ants everywhere. Well, they are said to never cross a chalk line. So get your chalk out and draw a line on the floor or wherever ants tend to march—see for yourself.

22) Use air-freshener to clean mirrors: It does a good job and better still, leaves a lovely smell to the shine.

23) When you get a splinter, reach for the scotch tape before resorting to tweezers or a needle. Simply put the scotch tape over the splinter, then pull it off. Scotch tape removes most splinters painlessly and easily.

24) NOW Look what you can do with Alka-Seltzer:

Clean a toilet—drop in two Alka-Seltzer tablets, wait twenty minutes, brush, and flush. The citric acid and effervescent action clean vitreous china.

Clean a vase—to remove a stain from the bottom of a glass vase or cruet, fill with water and drop in two Alka-Seltzer tablets.

Polish jewelry—drop two Alka-Seltzer tablets into a glass of water and immerse the jewelry for two minute.

Clean a thermos bottle—fill the bottle with water, drop in four Alka-Seltzer tablets, and let soak for an hour (or longer, if necessary).

Unclog a drain—clear the sink drain by dropping three Alka-Seltzer tablets down the drain followed by a cup of Heinz White Vinegar. Wait a few minutes, then run the hot water.

25) If your VCR has a year setting on it, which most do, you will not be able to use the programmed recording feature after 12/31/99. Don't throw it away. Instead, set it for the year 1972 as the days are the same as the year 2000. The manufacturers won't tell you. They want you to buy a new Y2K VCR.

For your information.edu

How to determine if a mirror is 2 way or not (Not a Joke!!!!!)

Not to scare you, but to make you aware.This was passed on by a policewoman who travels all over the states and gives seminars and techniques for business women.

HOW TO DETECT A 2-WAY MIRROR

When we visit toilets, bathrooms, hotel rooms, changing rooms, etc., how many of you know for sure that the seemingly ordinary mirror hanging on the wall is a real mirror, or actually a 2-way mirror (i.e., they can see you, but you can't see them)?

There have been many cases of people installing 2-way mirrors in female changing rooms. It is very difficult to positively identify the surface by just looking at it. So, how do we determine with any amount of certainty what type of mirror we are looking at? Just conduct this simple test: Place the tip of your fingernail against the reflective surface and if there is a GAP between your fingernail and the image of the nail, then it is a GENUINE mirror.

However, if your fingernail DIRECTLY TOUCHES the image of your nail, then BEWARE, FOR IT IS A 2-WAY MIRROR! So remember, every time you see a mirror, do the "fingernail test." It doesn't cost you anything. It is simple to do, and it might save you from getting "visually raped"!

Ladies: Share this with your girlfriends.

Men: Share this with your wives, daughters and/or girlfriend.

COFFEE.COM

Juan Valdez named his donkey after you.

You ski uphill.

You get a speeding ticket even when you're parked.

You speed walk in your sleep.

You have a bumper sticker that says: "Coffee drinkers are good in the sack."

You answer the door before people knock.

You haven't blinked since the last lunar eclipse.

You just completed another sweater and you don't know how to knit.

You grind your coffee beans in your mouth.

You sleep with your eyes open.

You have to watch videos in fast-forward.

The only time you're standing still is during an earthquake.

You can take a picture of yourself from ten feet away without using the timer.

You lick your coffeepot clean.

You spend every vacation visiting "Maxwell House."

You're the employee of the month at the local coffeehouse and you don't even work there.

You've worn out your third pair of tennis shoes this week.

Your eyes stay open when you sneeze.

You chew on other people's fingernails.

The nurse needs a scientific calculator to take your pulse.

Your T-shirt says, "Decaffeinated coffee is the devil's coffee."

Your so jittery that people use your hands to blend their margaritas.

You can type sixty words per minute with your feet.

You can jump-start your car without cables.

Cocaine is a downer.

All your kids are named "Joe."

You don't need a hammer to pound in nails.

Your only source of nutrition comes from "Sweet & Low."

You don't sweat, you percolate.

You buy milk by the barrel.

You've worn out the handle on your favorite mug.

You go to AA meetings just for the free coffee.

You walk twenty miles on your treadmill before you realize it's not plugged in.

You forget to unwrap candy bars before eating them.

Charles Manson thinks YOU need to calm down.

You've built a miniature city out of little plastic stirrers.

People get dizzy just watching you.

When you find a penny, you say, "Find a penny, pick it up. Sixty-three more, I'll have a cup."

You've worn the finish off your coffee table.

The Taster's Choice couple wants to adopt you.

Starbucks owns the mortgage on your house.

Your taste buds are so numb you could drink your lava lamp.

You're so wired, you pick up FM radio.

People can test their batteries in your ears.

Your life's goal IS to "amount to a hill of beans."

Instant coffee takes too long.

You channel surf faster without a remote.

When someone says. "How are you?", you say, "Good to the last drop."

You want to be cremated just so you can spend the rest of eternity in a coffee can.

You want to come back as a coffee mug in your next life.

Your birthday is a national holiday in Brazil.

You'd be willing to spend time in a Turkish prison.

You go to sleep just so you can wake up and smell the coffee.

You're offended when people use the word "brew" to mean beer.

You name your cats "Cream" and "Sugar."

You get drunk just so you can sober up.

You speak perfect Arabic without ever taking a lesson.

Your Thermos is on wheels.

Your lips are permanently stuck in the sipping position.

You have a picture of your coffee mug on your coffee mug.

You can outlast the Energizer bunny.

You short out motion detectors.

You have a conniption over spilled milk.

You don't even wait for the water to boil anymore.

Your nervous twitch registers on the Richter scale.

You think being called a "drip" is a compliment.

You don't tan, you roast.

You don't get mad, you get steamed.

Your three favorite things in life are.coffee before and coffee after.

Your lover uses soft lights, romantic music, and a glass of iced coffee to get you in the mood.

You can't even remember your second cup.

You help your dog chase its tail.

You soak your dentures in coffee overnight.

Your coffee mug is insured by Lloyds of London.

You introduce your spouse as your "Coffeemate."

You think CPR stands for "Coffee Provides Resuscitation."

Your first-aid kit contains two pints of coffee with an I.V. hookup.com

SERIOUS.EDU

I learned serious stuff too.edu

Something to think about!

A few years ago at the Seattle Special Olympics, nine contestants, all physically or mentally disabled, assembled at the starting line for the 100-yard dash. At the gun, they all started out, not exactly in a dash, but with a relish to run the race to the finish and win. All, that is, except one boy who stumbled on the asphalt, tumbled over a couple of times and began to cry. The other eight heard the boy cry. They slowed down and looked back. They all turned around and went back. Everyone of them.

One girl with Down's Syndrome bent down and kissed him and said, "This will make it better." All nine linked arms and walked across the finish line together. Everyone in the stadium stood, and the cheering went on for several minutes. People who were there are still telling the story. Why? Because deep down we know this one thing: What matters in this life is more than winning for ourselves. What truly matters in this life is helping others win, even if it means slowing down and changing our course.

Written By Mother Teresa.edu

People are often unreasonable, illogical,
and self-centered;
Forgive them anyway.
If you are kind, People may accuse you
of selfish, ulterior motives;
Be kind anyway.
If you are successful, you will win some
false friends and some true enemies;
Succeed anyway.

If you are honest and frank,
people may cheat you;
Be honest and frank anyway.
What you spend years building, someone
could destroy overnight;
Build anyway.
If you find serenity and happiness,
they may be jealous;
Be happy anyway.
The good you do today,
people will often forget tomorrow;
Do good anyway.
Give the world the best you have,
and it may never be enough;
Give the world the best you've got anyway.
You see, in the final analysis,
it is between you and God;
It was never between you and them anyway.

ATTITUDE DETERMINES ATTITUDE.edu

I woke up early today, excited over all I get to do before the clock strikes midnight. I have responsibilities to fulfill today. I am important. My job is to choose what kind of day I am going to have.

Today I can complain because the weather is rainy or I can be thankful that the grass is getting watered for free.

Today I can feel sad that I don't have more money or I can be glad that my finances encourage me to plan my purchases wisely and guide me away from waste.

Today I can grumble about my health or I can rejoice that I am alive.

Today I can lament over all that my parents didn't give me when I was growing up or I can feel grateful that they allowed me to be born.

Today I can cry because roses have thorns or I can celebrate that thorns have roses.

Today I can mourn my lack of friends or I can excitedly embark upon a quest to discover new relationships.

Today I can whine because I have to go to work or I can shout for joy because I have a job to do. I can complain because I have to go to school or eagerly open my mind and fill it with rich new tidbits of knowledge.

Today I can murmur dejectedly because I have to do housework or I can feel honored because the Lord has provided shelter for my mind, body and soul.

Today stretches ahead of me, waiting to be shaped. And here I am, the sculptor who gets to do the shaping.

With God's help, what today will be like is up to me. I get to choose what kind of day I will have!

INSTRUCTIONSFORLIFE.edu

1. Give people more than they expect and do it cheerfully.
2. Memorize your favorite poem.
3. Don't believe all you hear, spend all you have, or loaf all you want.
4. When you say, "I love you," mean it.
5. When you say, "I'm sorry," look the person in the eye.
6. Be engaged at least six months before you get married.
7. Believe in love at first sight.
8. Never laugh at anyone's dreams. People who don't have dreams don't have much.
9. Love deeply and passionately. You may get hurt, but it's the only way to live life completely.
10. In disagreements, fight fairly. No name-calling.
11. Don't judge people by their relatives, or by the life they were born into.
12. Teach yourself to speak slowly but think quickly.

13. When someone asks you a question you don't want to answer, smile and ask, "Why do you want to know?"
14. Take into account that great love and great achievements involve great risk.
15. Call your mother.
16. Say, "bless you" when you hear someone sneeze.
17. When you lose, don't lose the lesson.
18. Follow the three R's: Respect for self, Respect for others, Responsibility for all your actions.
19. Don't let a little dispute injure a great friendship.
20. When you realize you've made a mistake, take immediate steps to correct it.
21. Smile when picking up the phone. The caller will hear it in your voice.
22. Marry a person you love to talk to. As you get older, his/her conversational skills will be even more important.
23. Spend some time alone.
24. Open your arms to change but don't let go of your values.
25. Remember that silence is sometimes the best answer.
26. Read more books. Television is no substitute.
27. Live a good, honorable life. Then when you get older and think back, you'll be able to enjoy it a second time.
28. Trust in God but lock your car.
29. A loving atmosphere in your home is the foundation for your life. Do all you can to create a tranquil harmonious home.
30. In disagreements with loved ones, deal only with the current situation. Don't bring up the past.
31. Don't just listen to what someone is saying. Listen to why they are saying it.
32. Share your knowledge. It's a way to achieve immortality.
33. Be gentle with the earth.
34. Pray or meditate. There's immeasurable power in it.
35. Never interrupt when you are being flattered.

36. Mind your own business.
37. Don't trust anyone who doesn't close his/her eyes when you kiss.
38. Once a year, go someplace you've never been before.
39. If you make a lot of money, put it to use helping others while you are living. It is wealth's greatest satisfaction.
40. Remember that not getting what you want is sometimes a wonderful stroke of luck.
41. Learn the rules so you know how to break them properly.
42. Remember that the best relationship is one in which your love for each other exceeds your need for each other.
43. Judge your success by what you had to give up in order to get it.
44. Live with the knowledge that your character is your destiny.
45. Approach love and cooking with reckless abandon.

The following was written by Audrey Hepburn regarding "Beauty Tips".

For attractive lips, Speak words of kindness.

For lovely eyes, Seek out the good in people.

For a slim figure, Share your food with the hungry.

For beautiful hair, let a child run his or her fingers through it once a day.

For poise, Walk with the knowledge you'll never walk alone.

People, even more than things, have to be restored, renewed, revived, reclaimed, and redeemed; Never throw out anybody.

Remember, If you ever need a helping hand, you'll find one at the end of your arm. As you grow older, you will discover that you have two hands, one for helping yourself, the other for helping others.

The beauty of a woman is not in the clothes she wears, The figure that she carries, or the way she combs her hair. The beauty of a woman must be seen from in her eyes, because that is the doorway to her heart, the place where love resides.

The beauty of a woman is not in a facial mole, but the true beauty in a woman is reflected in her soul. It is the caring that she lovingly gives, the passion that she shows, And the beauty of a woman with passing years-only grows!

TO BE THANKFUL FOR.edu

The mess to clean after a party because it means I have been surrounded by friends.

The taxes I pay because it means that I'm employed.

The clothes that fit a little too snug because it means I have enough to eat.

My shadow who watches me work because it means I am out in the sunshine.

A lawn that needs mowing, windows that need cleaning and gutters that need fixing because it means I have home.

All the complaining I hear about our government because it means we have freedom of speech.

The space I find at the far end of the parking lot because it means I am capable of walking.

My huge heating bill because it means I am warm.

The lady behind me in church who sings off key because it means that I can hear.

The piles of laundry and ironing because it means I have clothes to wear.

Weariness and aching muscles at the end of the day because it means I have been productive.

The alarm that goes off in the early morning hours because it means that I'm alive.

Getting too much Email bogs me down but at least I know I have friends who are thinking of me.

COMPUTERS.COM

Subject: 15 Reasons you know you're part of the '00s.edu

15. You try to enter your password on the microwave.

14. You haven't played solitaire with a real deck of cards in years.

13. You have a list of 15 phone numbers to reach your family of 3.

12. You e-mail your son in his room to tell him that dinner is ready, and he e-mails you back "What's for dinner?"

11. Your daughter sells Girl Scout Cookies via her web site.

10. You chat several times a day with a stranger from South Africa, but you haven't spoken to your next door neighbor yet this year.

9. Your daughter just bought on CD all the records your college roommate used to play that you most despised.

8. Every commercial on television has a website address at the bottom of the screen.

7. You buy a computer and a week later it is out of date. And now sells for half the price you paid.

6. The concept of using real money, instead of credit or debit, to make a purchase is foreign to you.

5. Cleaning up the dining area means getting the fast food bags out of the of the back seat of your car.

4. Your reason for not staying in touch with family is that they do not have e-mail addresses.

3. You consider 2nd day air delivery painfully slow.

2. You refer to your dining room table as the flat filing cabinet. and the Number 1 sign that you've had too much of the 00's.

1. You hear most of your jokes via e-mail instead of in person.

KOSHER COMPUTERS.com

The Rabbi came over yesterday and we had a bris for my computer (ritual circumcision), taking a little piece off the tail of the mouse. If you or a friend are considering a kosher computer, you should know that there were some other changes, such as: I had to have two hard drives, one for fleyshedik business software and one for milchedik games.

Instead of getting a "General Protection Fault" error, my PC now gets "Ferklempt".

The Chanukah screen savers include "Flying Dreidels".

My PC also shuts down automatically at sundown on Friday evenings.

After my computer dies, I have to dispose of it within 24 hours.

My "Start" button has been replaced with a "Let's go! I'm not getting any younger!" button.

When disconnecting external devices from the back of my PC, I am instructed to "Remove the cable from the PC's tuchus".

The multimedia player has been renamed to "Nu, so play my music already!"

Internet Explorer has a spinning "Star of David" in the upper right corner.

I hear "Hava Nagila" during startup.

Microsoft Office now includes "A little byte of this, and a little byte of that."

When running "scandisk,", I am prompted with a "You want I should fix this?" message.

When my PC is working too hard, I occasionally hear a loud "Oy Gevalt!"

I saw a "monitor cleaning solution" from Manischewitz that advertises that it gets rid of the "schmutz and drek" on your monitor.

After 20 minutes of no activity, my PC goes "Schloffen".

Computer viruses can now be cured with some matzo ball chicken soup.

Y2K problems have been eliminated, but the impending Y6K problem promises to cause major tsoris.

LIFE BEFORE THE COMPUTER.com

An application was for employment
A program was a TV show
A cursor used profanity
A keyboard was a piano!

Memory was something that you lost with age
A CD was a bank account
And if you had a 3 1/2 inch floppy
You hoped nobody found out!

Compress was something you did to garbage
Not something you did to a file
And if you unzipped anything in public
You'd be in jail for awhile!

Log on was adding wood to a fire
Hard drive was a long trip on the road
A mouse pad was where a mouse lived
And a backup happened to your commode!

Cut—you did with a pocket knife
Paste you did with glue
A web was a spider's home
And a virus was the flu!

I guess I'll stick to my pad and paper
And the memory in my head
I hear nobody's been killed in a computer crash
But when it happens they wish they were dead!

PROVERBS FOR THE NEW MILLENNIUM.com

1. Home is where you hang your @.
2. The e-mail of the species is more deadly than the mail.
3. A journey of a thousand sites begins with a single click.
4. You can't teach a new mouse old clicks.
5. Great groups from little icons grow.
6. Speak softly and carry a cellular phone.
7. C:\ is the root of all directories.
8. Oh, what a tangled website we weave when first we practice.
9. Pentium wise, pen and paper foolish.
10. The modem is the message.
11. Too many clicks spoil the browse.
12. The geek shall inherit the earth.
13. There's no place like Home.
14. Don't byte off more than you can view.
15. Fax is stranger than fiction.
16. What boots up must come down.
17. Windows will never cease.
18. Virtual reality is its own reward.
19. Modulation in all things.
20. Give a man a fish and you feed him for a day;
Teach him to use the Net and he won't bother you for weeks.

Word Tip.
(1) Go to MS Word
(2) Type the phrase "I'd love to see you naked" (without the quotes)
(3) Highlight the whole phrase
(4) go to the tools menu
(5) choose thesaurus (Shift F7)

TOP 10 SIGNS THAT YOU KNOW IT'S TIME TO JOIN E-MAILERS ANONYMOUS.edu

10. You wake up at 3 a.m. to go to the bathroom, and check your e-mail on the way back to bed.

9. Your firstborn is named dotcom.

8. You turn off your modem and are suddenly filled with a feeling of emptiness, as if you just pulled the plug on a loved one.

7. You spend half of a plane trip with your laptop in your lap.and your child in the overhead compartment.

6. You decide to stay in college for an additional year or two, just for the free Internet access.

5. You find yourself typing "com" after every period.com

4. You refer to going to the bathroom as downloading.

3. You move into a new home and decide to netscape before you landscape.

2. You start tilting your head sideways to smile. :)

DRUM ROLL PLEASE

AND THE NO. 1 SIGN THAT YOU KNOW IT'S TIME TO JOIN E-MAILERS ANONYMOUS:

1. Immediately after reading this list, you e-mail it to someone or you write a book.

YADA.YADA.YADA.**THE END**.COM.EDU.ORG.GOV

or else I could fill the Library of Congress

AFTERWORD

If the world were 100 people
    There would be:
    57 Asians
    21 Europeans
    14 from North and South America.
    8 Africans
    52 would be female
    48 would be male
    70 would be nonwhite, 30 white
    59% of the entire world's wealth would belong to only 6 people and all
    6 would be
    citizens of the United States.
    80 would live in substandard housing
    70 would be unable to read
    50 would suffer from malnutrition
    1 would be near birth
    Only 1 would have a college education
    99 of them would not see these messages
    because only 1 would have a computer.
    That's why I wrote the book !!!!!!

0-595-10061-9

www.ingramcontent.com/pod-product-compliance
Lightning Source LLC
Chambersburg PA
CBHW021142070326
40689CB00043B/995